The New Pocket Guide XL

Tools for the Elimination of Waste!

SUSTAINING TO WORLD CLASS

DEMAND TOOLS

FLOW TOOLS

PEOPLE INVOLVEMENT

© 2010 by MCS Media, Inc.

All rights reserved. No part of this book may be reproduced or utilized in any form or by any means, electronic or mechanical, including photocopying, recording, or by any information storage and retrieval system, without permission in writing from the publisher.

ISBN 0-9770720-1-0

07 06 05 04 03   5 4 3 2 1

Contents

Acknowledgements v

Publisher's Message vii

How to Use *The New Lean Pocket Guide XL* ix

Lean Tool Usage Matrix xi

5S - Workplace Organization and Standardization 1

Buffer and Safety Stock 8

Cellular Layout: U-shaped 12

Continuous Flow (One-Piece Flow) 17

Cycle Time 19

Heijunka (Load Leveling) 22

Jidoka (Building Quality In) 27

Just-In-Time (JIT) 34

Kaizen Workshops 37

Kanban (Pull System) 41

Lean Metrics (OEE) 47

Lean Office (Paper File System)   **NEW!** 52

Lean Communications 64

Line Balancing 72

Mistake-Proofing (Poka-Yoke) 77

Origins of Lean 83

Paced Withdrawal 89

Perishable Tool Management   94

Pitch   99

Problem Solving Methodology   102

Product Quantity (PQ) Analysis and Part Routing Analysis 112

Quick Changeover (QCO)   116

Runner   120

Sequence to Lean Implementation   123

Six Sigma   **NEW!**   127

Standard Work   133

Storyboard   138

Takt Time   140

Total Productive Maintenance (TPM)   143

Value Stream Management (VSM)   149

Value Stream Mapping   156

Visual Factory   165

Waste   172

Waste Audit   **NEW!**   181

Glossary   **NEW!**   186

Acknowledgements

The New Lean Pocket Guide XL represents the input of a select group of lean and quality experts and places at your fingertips a concise reference on the key tools of lean implementation. This work could not have been completed without their commitment: their expertise and experience will prove invaluable to any company embarked on the lean journey. Now we have added new sections to enhance the previous best selling edition of *The Lean Pocket Guide.* I wish to thank each of them individually:

Bob Angeli, VP Operations, Genzink Steel
Holland, Michigan
25 years of lean implementation
Sensei

Tom Fabrizio, Consultant and Author, *Value Stream Management Learning Tool, Lean Tooling, 5S, 5S for Safety, 5S for the Office*
Portland, Oregon
20 years of lean implementation
Sensei

Roger Kremer, Manager, Global Manufacturing Excellence, Eaton Corporation
Jackson, Michigan
30 years of lean implementation
Sensei

Tom Melcher, Consultant and Author, *Lean Sigma, Six Sigma for the Front Line*
Grand Rapids, Michigan
25 years of lean and quality implementation

Kim DeForest, Trainer/Facilitator, Eaton Corporation
Jackson, Michigan
10 years of lean implementation

Joe Singer, Training Director, Lacks Enterprises, Inc.
Grand Rapids, Michigan
10 years of lean implementation

Amy Rossi, Industrial Engineering Manager, The Oakwood Group
Taylor, Michigan
10 years of lean implementation

Don Tapping
Publisher

Publisher's Message

After countless years of training and hiring consultants in the area of lean implementation, I realized that the people who actually implement lean—those on the shop floor, searching for ways to improve an area, process or work standard—had nothing truly practical to use on a daily basis in their jobs. *The New Lean Pocket Guide XL* is meant to fill that gap. It frees you from bulky manuals, books, or videos, providing the information you need at the right place, at the right time and in the right amount.

This new version includes digital photos of lean practices for many of the topics. Over 30 photos have been placed through this guide to allow you a further insight into the application of particular tools. We have also included a chapter on Lean Office and Six Sigma. Most importantly, due to *your* suggestions, we have included a Waste Audit and a Glossary of lean terms.

The essential lean tools are all here, functionally described and illustrated for ease of adaptation and usage to:

• Identify and eliminate waste quickly and efficiently
• Increase communication at all levels of the organization
• Reduce costs and improve quality
• Begin improvements immediately and empower workers to make improvements themselves

Bolster your lean transformation with *The New Lean Pocket Guide XL*. Developed for both managers and shop floor operators, here's a graphically rich, ready reference on lean manufacturing methods to reduce costs, improve quality, deliver products on time—and provide you with the necessary content allowing you to remain globally competitive in the 21st century!

Don Tapping

Thanks for the love, patience, and support from my wife, Kim, and from my sons, Mark, Christopher, and Stephen.

How to Use *The New Lean Pocket Guide XL*

The New Lean Pocket Guide XL is designed for use as a convenient, quick reference as you learn and implement lean manufacturing tools and techniques. It provides valuable insight into the nuances of lean. You can put your finger on any entry within a matter of seconds! And it is most definitely meant for the shop floor!

Find the right tool for the right lean initiative by using the:

- **Table of Contents** providing the listing of tools, techniques, and supporting documentation in alphabetical order.
- **Lean Tool Usage Matrix** organizing the lean tools and concepts relative to various aspects of lean implementation. For instance, if you are working on page xi and xii determining customer demand, you would be referencing buffer and safety stock, cycle time, etc.
- **Waste Audit** providing guidelines for the team to ask questions regarding waste relative to their value stream.
- **Glossary** providing a definition of the various lean tools and concepts.

What do the climber icons signify?

The lean journey is similar to climbing a mountain. It requires people (climbers), support (teamwork), and effective use of correct tools and procedures (grappling hooks, ropes, etc.). Overall, it requires accomplishing a goal. In lean the goal is to eliminate waste, and thus reduce non value-added time!

Getting Started: An important, if not critical, step is to select the right tool for the lean project or improvement initiative. When you see this climber, expect a brief description of the tool's purpose, who is mainly responsible for doing it, how long will it take to complete, and the benefits it will provide.

Making Progress: When you see this icon, expect to find detailed steps in the implementation and use of this tool. This is the action phase that provides you with the step-by-step information for you to ensure the tool is used properly.

Achieving Goal: When you see this icon, expect to benefit from the many lessons learned over the years by the authors of this pocket guide. And at this point, you have accomplished your goal and must now link this lean concept to other improvements within the organization.

Lean Tool Usage Matrix

The overall goal of *The New Lean Pocket Guide XL* is to inform you how lean tools and concepts can be utilized to eliminate waste. The further you define, analyze, and attack sources of waste, the more you will find yourself utilizing these tools within a proper sequence of implementation—and the further you will travel down the road to lean.

The Lean Tool Usage Matrix on the next page organizes the tools and concepts relative to various aspects of lean implementation. The importance of this is threefold.

1. It ensures tools are utilized within a systematic implementation plan. For example, you would not want to use line balancing if you have not established accurate and reliable cycle times.
2. It raises awareness that many tools are utilized in the planning and enabling of lean.
3. It communicates that visual controls and Jidoka should be overriding themes throughout lean implementation.

Use the matrix as a guide reference, checklist, or template for brainstorming. It will help you apply the right tool, at the right time, in the right way!

Lean Tool Usage Matrix						
LEAN TOOL	PLAN/ ENABLE	DEMAND	FLOW	LEVELING	VISUAL CONTROL	GENERAL
5S	X					
Buffer and Safety Stock		X				
Cellular Layout			X			
Continuous Flow			X			
Cycle Time		X				
Heijunka (Leveling)				X	X	
Mistake-Proofing					X	
Just-In-Time			X			
Kaizen	X					
Kanban					X	
Lean Metrics	X					
Lean Office	X	X	X	X	X	
Lean Communications	X					
Line Balancing			X			
Mistake-Proofing					X	
Origins of Lean						X
Paced Withdrawal				X		
Perishable Tool Management						X
Pitch		X				
PQ Analysis		X				
Problem Solving	X					X
Quick Changeover			X			
Runner				X		
Sequence to Lean Implementation	X					
Six Sigma	X	X	X	X	X	X
Standard Work		X			X	
Storyboard	X				X	
Takt Time		X				
Total Productive Maintenance		X				
Value Stream Management	X					
Value Stream Mapping	X					
Visual Factory					X	
Waste						X

5S -
Workplace Organization and Standardization

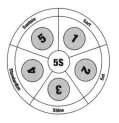

Why use it?

To ensure work areas are systematically kept clean and organized, ensuring employee safety, and providing for the foundation on which to build a lean system.

1st S—for **sorting** the necessary from the unnecessary
2nd S—for planning the best place to **set** items in order
3rd S—for **shining**, cleaning and identifying items
4th S—for creating and setting the **standard** for cleanliness
5th S—for establishing the discipline to **sustain** the first 4 S's over time

Who does it?

- A temporary lean team is normally established to initiate and monitor the 5S implementation.
- All employees must participate for the system to be effective.

How long will it take to do?

Depending on the area, each "S" could take only a few hours to begin with, then minutes per day/per employee to maintain.

What does it do?

Provides a structure and steps for workplace organization, order, and cleanliness. This is accomplished by:

- Putting a team of workers in control of their own workspace
- Helping a team focus on the causes and elimination of wastes
- Establishing standards of housekeeping, storage, and visual communication
- Preparing the work area for lean implementation
- Showing customers that a clean shop is important and thus conveying pride in product quality
- Improving employee morale by making the area safe, clean, and enjoyable to work in

How do you do it?

A cross-functional team is assembled and a target area chosen. Workers from the area are key in making this project a success. 5S can be used throughout the organization—*both in the plant and office.*

Consider utilizing "5S Gold Stars" as a visual aid as each step is completed. You would want to reward the team/cell area once all steps have been completed. After that, conduct monthly reviews or audits to ensure that 5S is being sustained.

1st S - Sort through and sort out

This is the weeding out of items within the target area that have not been used for a period of time or are not expected to be used.

---

1. The team defines the purpose for an area and is used as a basis for which items are essential in step 2.
2. The team agrees on the items that are not essential to the target area.
3. The items are then "red tagged."

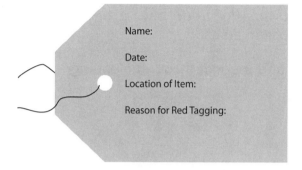

Name:

Date:

Location of Item:

Reason for Red Tagging:

4. Tagged items are then moved to a staging area (a place where decisions about the item will be made). Create one if you do not have one.
5. Leaders and/or managers are to determine the disposition of tagged items. This may include: return to area, find a new home, dispose, and/or repair.
6. Begin to determine the best area for remaining items.
7. Put up a project bulletin board for communication to other employees and prominently display before and after photographs.

2nd S - Set things in order and set limits

1. Begin implementation of storage plans, mark off floors, label and identify everything.
2. Create a standard of the target area, something to refer to if an item is out of place: a) it should be obvious if something is missing; and b) each item should be labeled so that it is obvious where it belongs.
3. Monitor the area for a few days after implementation for input or problem areas.

3rd S - Shine and inspect through cleaning

Clean the target area. A good cleaning is required. But more than that, from now on, cleaning is seen as a form of equipment and safety inspection.

Example: *Consider the case of the machine operator who started wondering if she could stop the coolant from leaking, since she was now the one cleaning it up. As it turned out they were over-filling it every time! And with the wrong coolant!*

Initial Cleaning Plan

Task	Location	Who	When	Materials	Tools

4th S - Standardize

1. On a sheet (sample on previous page) list areas that need regular cleaning and/or inspection.

2. List on same sheet frequency of cleaning and/or inspection (time of day, weekly, monthly, etc.).

3. Identify who is responsible for cleaning area and time. (You may wish to rotate cleaning assignments weekly or monthly.)

Standard Inspection Sheet
Have you removed dust, dirt, oil, etc. from tools?
Have you put all tools back into their storage place?
Have you put inventory back into where it belongs?
Have you restored jigs, dies, etc. in proper place?
Have you wiped the machines down and checked or leaks?
Did you check for any loose nuts or bolts?
Did you check for needed bulbs or tubes?
Have you cleaned the bench?
Did you remove items that are not needed?
Is the area generally clean?
Have you swept and mopped the floor?

4. Post the cleaning schedule in the target area (preferably laminated, so that it can be initialed and re-used). Tip: this is a form of Total Productive Maintenance (TPM).

5. Post before and after photos in area to showcase success.

6. After photos become part of the standard for the target area.

5th S - Sustain through inspection

1. It is the job of management to enforce a standard and inspect to the standard.

2. Enforce the standard by rewarding and recognizing adherence to the standard and correcting behavior and/or the process if standard is deteriorating.

Key Points to Remember

• 5S must become part of everyone's job.
• The better you implement the first S—sort—the less there will be to set in order and shine. So, when you do the first S, do a complete job. Don't rush through it.
• A trained 5S facilitator or instructor should lead the early 5S projects.
• Before-and-after photos should be posted in areas as visual examples of success.
• Advertise successes to develop excitement that rapid and radical change is possible.
• Award "5S Gold Stars" as progress is made through the 5S process.

- Management's role in the Sustain step must be preformed to prevent deterioration.
- Implement, implement, implement!

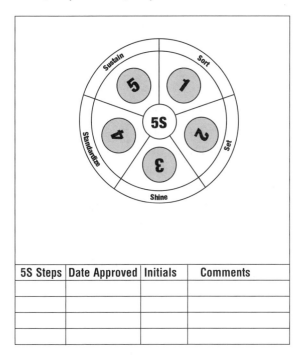

5S Steps	Date Approved	Initials	Comments

5S can "WOW" your customers if it is done correctly.

Audits should be done regularly.

Buffer and Safety Stock

Why use it?

The customer always comes first. When they order something, you *must* be able to ship it or risk losing that customer. If for some unforeseen reason you cannot produce what the customer wants, your backup plan is to arrange for buffer and safety stock.

Buffer stock. Stock made available between processes to meet takt time due to variations in upstream or downstream cycle times. Buffer stock smoothes out variations between processes, thus assuring that overall takt time is maintained at a consistent rate. This also protects the customer from variation. If located at the last process prior to shipment, it would be referred to as finished goods buffer stock.

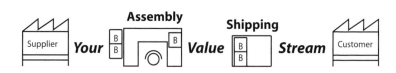

Safety stock. Goods made available to protect takt time while making process changes or improvements. Safety stock is utilized due to major internal failure (fire, machine shutdown, injury, power disruption, weather catastrophe, etc.). Safety stock should be under lock and key. A stringent process is necessary when safety stock is used, and it should be recorded. Safety stock must be rotated to prevent aging.

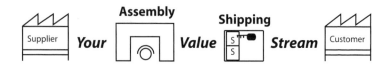

Who does it?

The calculation and determination of safety and buffer stock amounts should be done by the lean team, along with someone from materials and/or planning, and approved by higher levels of management.

How long will it take to do?

Approximately one hour to gather information and determine the inventory level. This also allows time for discussion. To implement buffer and safety stock controls and kanbans would normally take a few hours to days, depending on the team's focus. Both safety and buffer stock should be adjusted regularly as historical performance data becomes available.

What does it do?

Maintains takt time of overall process so that customer demand is consistently met by shielding customer from internal process variation.

 How do you do it?

Buffer stock

1. Select a process that is experiencing part shortages.
2. Analyze upstream process variation: average downtime.
3. Quantity in buffer stock must span average downtime period.

Finished goods buffer stock

1. Choose a particular product—one product at a time.
2. In this case we are deciding on buffer stock. Determine the variation of what the customer demand has been for the past 2 or 3 months. For example:

Week	Amount
1	910
2	740
3	720
4	810
5	820
6	880
7	785
8	610
9	710
10	725
11	850
12	740

3. Take the highest volume, subtract from that the daily demand. This will be the number of units you must have on hand to meet the customer demand.

In the example shown above, the product's history is shown for twelve weeks.

- The average weekly withdrawal is 775 units.
- The most the customer has taken above the average is 135 units.
- This occurred in week 1.
- **Therefore, the buffer will be set at 135 units.**

Safety stock

Safety stock is sized the same as buffer stock, but with little to no process downtime or variation history. The size of the safety stock must be based on predictions of the downtime of the process *and* the risk the organization is willing to endure.

Key Points to Remember

- Safety and buffer stock must be kept separate. Both must be logged in and out. Safety stock should be kept under lock and key, and only the plant manager or production manager will release it. This will bring about awareness of manufacturing inefficiency.
- Safety and buffer stocks should be viewed as compromises to a lean system. Kaizen activities should constantly be working on eliminating both of these.
- Establishing buffer and safety stock also allows you to meet demand without scrambling to schedule overtime sporadically. Instead, you can *plan* when you will run overtime.
- Safety and buffer stock are intended to protect the customers; buffer stock for internal customers, safety stock for external customers.

Safety stock as finished goods should be tracked and stored separately.

Cellular Layout: U-shaped

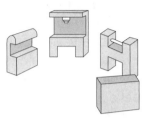

Why use it?

To create workplace efficiency and flexibility with respect to equipment, people, and part presentation.

Who does it?

The lean team will work with the operator in a kaizen event.

How long will it take to do?

Existing process: two to four hours to develop a plan to redesign into a U-shaped cell. Four hours to two days to rearrange equipment. The physical movement will depend on equipment complexity.

New process: days to weeks, as equipment and process is designed in conjunction with the product.

What does it do?

- Ensures most efficient layout for worker
- Ensures the shortest distance of part movement
- Allows for maximum flexibility via sharing of work elements with processes behind and diagonal to one another
- It is the foundation of—and it enforces—one-piece and/or small-lot flow

- Connects processes with the same volume requirements
- Reduces the amount of floor space required
- Allows flexible output rate by adding or removing operators

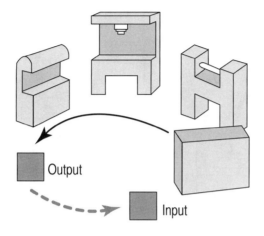

Output

Input

How do you do it?

1. Draw layout of equipment flowing counterclockwise. Consider the layout of equipment for each process.
2. Locate machine next to the equipment for the preceding process so that one-piece or small-lot manufacturing can occur.
3. Create various Standard Work Charts for high, low, and average takt time scenarios. (See **Standard Work**)
   - This tells managers how many workers are needed for differing takt times.
   - This will allow additional workers to adapt quickly to differing takt times. (See example next page)

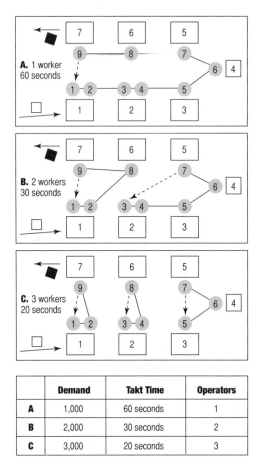

	Demand	Takt Time	Operators
A	1,000	60 seconds	1
B	2,000	30 seconds	2
C	3,000	20 seconds	3

4. Cycle times of equipment of slowest machine must be increased to shortest takt time or less. Ideally, all equipment cycle times are balanced.

5. Plan how material can be delivered from outside the cell so it is available to operators inside the cells (slides, rails, rollers, etc.).

6. Use automation within the cell only for safety and ergonomics, or when cycle time of a certain piece of the process must be improved in order to meet takt time.

Other considerations are:

- Determine preventive maintenance requirements and allocate time for this to occur daily (TPM).
- Ensure that maintenance procedures and schedules are visually posted.
- Establish quick changeover procedures so there is ease of converting from one product to another.
- Standardize changeover procedures so that everyone understands them, thus minimizing machine downtime.
- Machines and worktables should be on rollers whenever possible for ease of re-arrangement in future kaizens.
- Do not hard wire equipment. Use hoses and flex cables dropped from the ceiling. This speeds re-arrangement.
- Cross-train all operators to operate all machines and perform any of the different standardized work jobs for the one-, two-, or three-operator scenarios.

Key Points to Remember

- Do not group machines by type.
- Usually, the cells operate in a *counterclockwise* direction.
- Arrange cells according to processing sequence.
- Design cells for operators standing up and ensure operator movement does not conflict if more than one operator is in the cell.
- Review the sequence of steps at an individual operation to eliminate excess material handling.
- Ensure that defects can be immediately detected (poka-yoke).
- Ensure the operator can operate all the machines within the cell.

U-shaped cells should be well-organized to maximize one-piece or small-lot flow.

U-shaped work areas can also be effective in administrative areas.

Continuous Flow
(One-Piece Flow)

```
            ┌──────┐
            │Kanban│
    ┌───────┴──────┴──┐
    │      Part       │
    └──┬──────────────┘
       │        ┌──────┐
       │        │Kanban│
    ┌──┴────────┴──────┴──┐
    │        Part          │
    └──────────────────────┘
```

 Why use it?

To move product throughout the value stream one piece at a time with no inventory and waste.

Who does it?

The lean team will design and utilize lean tools, but everyone will be responsible for maintaining the standards that exist to ensure continuous flow occurs.

How long will it take to do?

Days, weeks or months, depending on the complexity of the value stream and the resources committed.

What does it do?

The advantages of continuous flow are:

- Ability to shorten lead times by having no or minimum work-in-process inventory
- Ease in identifying defects and/or problems before they get to the customer
- Availability of multi-functional workers when they are most needed
- Ability to utilize standard work to maintain flow with less experienced operators

How do you do it?

1. Set up U-shaped cell where it can be accommodate such an arrangement. When constraints prohibit this type of layout, an S-shape, L-shape or straight line can be utilized. (See **Cellular Layout**)

2. Layout equipment such that each process can be located next to the proceeding process so that one-for-one or small-lot manufacturing can occur.

3. Balance cycle times of equipment/assembly operations for the entire cell.

4. Consider advanced technology, preventive maintenance, and quick changeovers as you design the cell.

Key Points to Remember

- Continually work to shorten lead times.
- Continually work to minimize work-in-progress.
- Work to identify and eliminate problems as they arise.
- Allow for multi-functional workers where they are needed.

Cycle Time

Why use it?

To compare with takt time and to determine the number of workers needed to complete an operation or process. It is required for developing standard work.

Who does it?

Anyone familiar with the operation or process in question can time it.

How long will it take to do?

15 to 30 minutes depending on the complexity of the process.

What does it do?

Cycle time is the amount of time for a task to be completed. Cycle time should not be confused with takt time. Cycle time is the rate of the process.

Cycle time:

- Allows for a clear understanding of how many operators are needed (if takt time is known)
- Should be utilized in the Standard Work Combination Table
- Allows combining a number of cycles with one operator in order to fully utilize that operator over the entire takt time

There are two types of cycle time:

- **Individual cycle time**—the rate of completion of an individual operation; for example, packing, or welding.
- **Total cycle time**—the rate of completion of a process of operation. You calculate this number by adding together all individual cycle times in a given process.

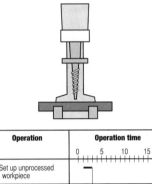

Operation	Operation time
	0 5 10 15
1. Set up unprocessed workpiece	
2. Turn switch on	
3. Feed (automatic)	
Total	Human work / machine work 3 8

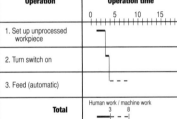

How do you do it?

To determine how many workers are required for a task:

1. Operator cycle times are obtained by adding all tasks in an individual operation.

Operator 1

Elmt.	Desc.	Time
1	Cut	9.2
2	Bore	5.1
3	Tube	4.3
4	Clip	3.8

Total time 22.4 sec.

Operator 2

Elmt.	Desc.	Time
1	Pin	7.2
2	Key	6.9
3	Link	5.1

Total time 19.2 sec.

Operator 3

Elmt.	Desc.	Time
1	Pack	3.9
2	#2 Pin	6.8
3	De-burr	5.7

Total time 16.4 sec.

2. Add the operator cycle times to obtain the total cycle time.

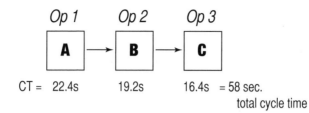

Operator 1: cycle time = 22.4 sec.

Operator 2: cycle time = 19.2 sec.

Operator 3: cycle time = 16.4 sec.

3. Calculate takt time. Remember, you calculate takt time by dividing available production time by total daily quantity required. (See **Takt Time**)

$$\frac{28{,}800 \text{ sec}}{960 \text{ units}} = 30 \text{ second takt time}$$
(Customer wants 1 unit every 30 sec.)

4. Divide the total cycle time by the takt time. This will give you the total number of workers required for the tasks.

$$\text{\# of operators needed} = \frac{58 \text{ sec. (total cycle time)}}{30 \text{ second (takt time)}} = 1.93 \text{ operators}$$

Key Points to Remember

- Determining the optimal number of workers is called line balancing. It is the process by which you evenly distribute the work elements among all operators.
- When determining the optimal number of workers required:
  - If decimal is greater than .5, round up
  - If decimal is less than .5, round down
  - Utilize kaizen to reduce cycle times where you can

Heijunka (Load Leveling)

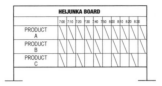

Why use it?

To enable you to meet varying customer demand without varying the workload on the manufacturing process. This is especially useful when a mix of models or several variations (colors, options) of a product exist.

Who does it?

A cross-functional team made up of production, material planning, quality control, and floor personnel.

How long will it take to do?

Two to six months.

What does it do?

- Levels production in a value stream by volume and variety
- Reduces inventory levels
- Enables you to establish a true pull system
- Takes the paced withdrawal system, utilizing pitch, and breaks it into units based on the volume and variety of product being produced

How do you do it?

1. Calculate takt time.

$$\text{Takt time} = \frac{\text{Available daily production time}}{\text{Total daily quantity required}} = \frac{\text{Time}}{\text{Volume}}$$

2. Determine pitch for each product.

Pitch is the time required to produce and pack the box, pallet or whatever meets the customer's instructions for shipping.

Multiply takt time by pack-out quantity and divide by 60 seconds.

$$\text{Pitch} = \frac{\text{Takt time x pack-out quantity}}{60 \text{ seconds}}$$

Important point: Each product will probably have a different pitch. But when you create a production sequence (below) it will be based on the smallest container or pitch. The following example will clarify this.

Assume 3 products, A, B and C. Takt time is 60 seconds. Pack-out quantity is different for each product:

Pack-out quantities:
Product A = 10 pieces per box
Product B = 15 pieces per box
Product C = 20 pieces per box

Pitch calculation:

Product A =
10 minutes (60 sec T.T.) x 10 pieces/box) / (60 sec)

Product B =
15 minutes (60 sec T.T.) x 15 pieces/box) / (60 sec)

Product C =
20 minutes (60 sec T.T.) x 20 pieces/box) / (60 sec)

3. Create a production sequence.

Since the smallest pitch time is 10 minutes, the time sequence on the heijunka box will be as follows, in 10-minute sequences.

7:00   7:10   7:20   7:30   7:40   7:50 etc.

If breaks are given, but production is not affected, then the sequence can stay the same. Breaks that affect the sequence must have the board show it.

So a 20 minute lunch from 11:30 to 11:50 will be shown like this in the sequence, starting at 11:10:

11:10   11:20   *Lunch*   *Lunch*   11:50   12:00

4. Create a production sequence table.

A production sequence table is a matrix showing when each product needs to be packed, at what time, and in what quantities. This table gives you the whole story of the customer pull at a glance, and should be posted at the heijunka box because it also shows the sequence of the kanbans. It should be recalculated as customer demand changes.

Production Sequence Table

	7:00	7:10	7:20	7:30	7:40	7:50	8:00	8:10	8:20	8:30
Prod A (10 pcs)										
Prod B (15 pcs)										
Prod C (20 pcs)										

5. Create a heijunka box.

The heijunka box, or leveling box, is a physical device to level production volume and variety over a specified period of time. The load is leveled with consideration for the most efficient use of people and equipment. In a lean system this is the *only* place to input information on daily production requirements of the day.

In a sense, the heijunka box is like a mailbox for production, and the runner is the mailman. Kanban cards are placed in the box in packing slip sequence at the specified pitch increment.

HEIJUNKA BOX										
	7:00	7:10	7:20	7:30	7:40	7:50	8:00	8:10	8:20	8:30
PRODUCT A										
PRODUCT B										
PRODUCT C										

6. Put the heijunka box into operation.

This requires a runner or material handler. (See **Runner**) In addition, you may need to negotiate with your suppliers regarding delivery frequencies, quantities, and other requirements (container size, durability, etc.).

Key Points to Remember

• If you produce a variety of products, load leveling may be the key to establishing a pull system in your facility. Load leveling uses paced withdrawal based on pitch, but breaks it into units based on the volume and variety of the product being produced.

• A heijunka box should be set up so that there will be one row for each customer (or for each color) for each product.

• The box will have one column for each time pitch increment—if it is 10 minutes, there will be one column for every 10 minutes.

• There should be no more than one kanban per slot on the heijunka box.

• The row levels on the box should include pieces per bin and color of product.

Heijunka boards or boxes should be centrally located to ensure the most efficient route for the runner or supervisor.

Administrative areas can also use a mailbox system for work and/or service requests.

Jidoka (Building Quality In)

Broken drill bit
Workpiece
Spring
Alarm lamp (andon)

Why use it?

To achieve the appropriate level of automation that detects defects and halts when a defect is found. This level of automation is less costly than full automation and prevents defects from being passed on in the process.

Who does it?

Small, focused, cross-functional teams with engineering resources and a member with mistake-proofing (poka-yoke) experience.

How long will it take to do?

A cell, workstation or line can take 2 to 6 months to complete. Implementation times decrease as the team gains understanding of the concept and experience in implementing it.

What does it do?

This concept will allow for:
- Incorporating mistake-proofing devices so that machines detect and prevent mistakes from occurring and will not allow operator to proceed
- Applying mistake-proofing to assembly operations so that mistakes are detected immediately and corrective measures taken, with little or no down time
- Creating the necessary checks and balances in the front offices to ensure paper work is correct the first time

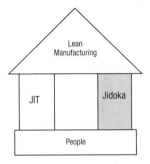

 How do you do it?

There are four steps in developing Jidoka, or "automation with a human touch," and each of them is concerned with the relationship between people and machines.

The 4 Steps to Jidoka

1. **Analysis:** Study the process—how much work people do, and how much work machines do.

2. **Mechanization:** Some portion of the manual work is taken over by a machine.

3. **Automation:** At this step, manual labor is taken over by the machine. But there is no way of knowing if there are any mistakes.

4. **Jidoka:** In this stage the machine *will* detect if there is an error and will shut itself off. In its most advanced applications, the machine will also correct the problem.

---

1. Analysis

Study the process—how much work people do, and how much machines do. Calculate a percentage. Draw a process flowchart.

2. Mechanization

Mechanization means leaving part of the manual operation to a worker. Work is shared between worker and machine. There are many levels of mechanization.

Example:

In this case, a wood plate came to a workstation, already cut to the proper size. The worker's job was to drill 4 holes in that plate (which constituted the bottom of the part), in the proper place, and screw a top into the plate (the top already had the screws in place). He used an electric hand drill for both operations.

The job looked like this, with a total cycle time of 155 seconds:

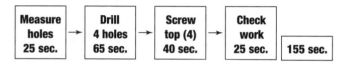

With mechanization, the following improvements were sustained:

• An automatic drill with 4 bits was purchased.
• With this drill the holes are already pre-measured, which eliminates the measurement step and 25 seconds from the cycle time.
• The worker only needs to place the plate under the drill (5 sec.)—a foot press operates it.
• All 4 holes are drilled simultaneously (10 sec.).
• The same drill has 4 additional bits on an easily hand-operated turning action. The bits to screw the top are already in the drill. It takes only 10 seconds to change bits.
• All 4 screws are screwed simultaneously (5 sec.).
• The reduced motion is easier on the worker's back—he or she is much less prone to injury.
• The drill bits are now being used correctly and have a longer life time. *And cycle time for the job is now 30 seconds!*

3. Automation

At this step, all manual labor is taken over by the machine. The worker just sets the job at the machine and presses a switch to begin the job. The worker can walk away at this point, but there is a problem: there is no way of knowing whether mistakes occur.

Example:

Using the previous example, let's say that the plant automated the drilling operation. That would involve the following:

- After the plate was cut, it would be put on a conveyer by the previous operation and brought to the drill.
- The machine, not the worker, would automatically place the plate under the drill.
- The machine would automatically drill the 4 holes.
- The machine, not the worker, would change the bits.
- The machine would automatically convey, place and screw the top.
- The machine would automatically send the completed piece on its way.
- The advantage might be that you can allow your worker to go somewhere else. The disadvantage is that this is much more expensive than partial automation or mechanization, and there is no one around to check quality.

4. Jidoka

At this stage the worker sets up the job, turns on the switch, and leaves. In this case *the machine will detect* if there is an error and will either shut itself off or correct the problem. It will also signal the event with bells, lights, or some detection system.

Example:

As mentioned earlier, it does no good to separate the worker from the machine if there is a chance that the machine will start producing defective products in the worker's absence. The solution is mistake-proofing devices. (See **Mistake-Proofing**)

How to Prevent Defects in Hole Drilling

The figure below shows an example of a mistake-proofing device used in drilling operations. Before improvement, this drilling machine, which uses 4 drill bits to simultaneously drill 4 places in the plate, experienced occasional defects due to broken drill bits, drilling omissions, and incomplete drilling. The plant had to inspect every piece, which took a great deal of time.

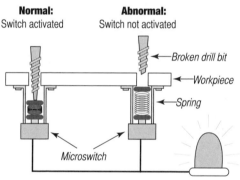

After the improvement, a microswitch was installed under each drill hole. If any of the 4 microswitches is not pressed during the operation, the machine stops itself, and a red alarm light, called an andon light, automatically comes on to alert the worker that there is a problem.

How to Prevent Defects in Assembly

The example we have been using is unique in that it is both a machining and assembly example. The assembly portion of the operation, where the top is screwed to the bottom, was not always done correctly or at times not at all. Before improvement, a worker would have to check the operation out periodically to make sure everything was running smoothly.

The mistake-proofing device consists of a photoelectric switch that reflects a light beam off a 1 inch by 2 inch section on the top of the part, which is shiny enough to create a reflection (where the bottom is not). The switch uses the reflection to detect whether the top has been attached; if it has not, a buzzer sounds and an andon light comes on.

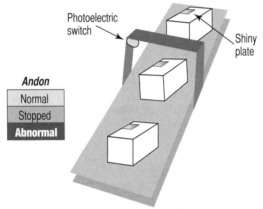

If the product does not bear a shiny plate, the andon is lit, a buzzer is sounded, and the line stops.

 ### Key Points to Remember

- Jidoka is not a one-step process.
- Jidoka is based on the practical use of automation to mistake-proof the detection of defects and free up workers to perform multiple tasks within work cells.
- Jidoka can be applied to virtually any process.
- Jidoka is different than automation. It is accomplished slowly, systematically, and inexpensively. It ensures that machines do only value-adding work.
- Implementing Jidoka reduces cycle time and prevents wastes such as waiting, transport, inspection, and defects.
- Jidoka should be implemented in simple forms before first attempting a full-scale error-proofed application.

- Moves "appropriate" (i.e., dull, dirty, dangerous, or critical operations) human work to machines. It is called "automation with a human touch."
- You must practice Jidoka to become proficient at it.

Just-In-Time (JIT)

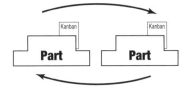

Why use it?

To establish a system of manufacturing and supplying products precisely at the right time, in the right amount, with neither defects nor waste.

Who does it?

1. A lean team is normally established to determine what areas will benefit from this philosophy—while realizing that it cannot be established overnight.
2. All employees must participate for the system to be effective.
3. Managers must understand and promote JIT over the long term for it to succeed!

How long will it take to do?

This is a long-term philosophy change.

What does it do?

Just-In-Time provides three basic elements to change a company's production system.

Continuous flow will:
- Typically utilize cellular concepts
- Allow material to flow from operation to operation without delay
- Improve worker-to-worker communication
- Enhance defect detection

Takt time will:
• Set the pace of the entire operation

The **pull system** (kanban) will:
• Allow material/products to flow without any inventory, or with a bare minimum of in-process inventory
• Reduce lead times and inventory carrying costs
• Reinforce the importance of 100 percent quality

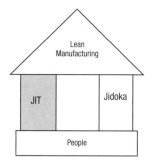

How do you do it?

1. Takt time is used in conjunction with standard work to illustrate the timing sequence of production for continuous flow.
2. Utilizing continuous flow principles will connect processes with balanced cycle times/volumes so that products can be produced at a steady pace. U-shaped cells can be used to accomplish this. (See **Cellular Layout**)
3. Utilizing the pull system ensures that product arrives at the correct location and in the correct amount, via signal cards called kanbans.
4. Use JIT as a concept to work toward when constructing a future-state value stream map. (See **Value Stream Mapping**)

Key Points to Remember

- The goal of JIT is to provide internal and external customers with quality products in a very specific way:
  - *Only* those units ordered
  - Just *when* they are needed
  - In the *exact amount* needed
  - With *no* defects
- This encompasses not only finished goods, but all material delivered to the next user or to an internal customer within the order-to-delivery process.
- JIT is part of a larger program and must be handled that way. People are what make it work!
- Gather implementation ideas from the workers.
- Think "the entire process," not just a single operation.
- JIT can be accomplished with little or no expense.
- Train, train, and train some more!

Kaizen Workshops

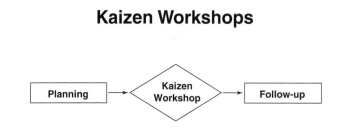

Why use it?
To quickly improve a specific area utilizing lean tools/concepts.

Who does it?
A cross-functional team made up of production, material planning, and quality control.

How long will it take to do?
- 3 to 5 days is a common kaizen workshop schedule.
- Complex kaizen workshops can take up to 2 months to complete:
  - 2 to 4 weeks of planning
  - The actual kaizen workshop lasts 3 to 5 days
  - Follow-up tasks are completed in 3 to 4 weeks

What does it do?

- Quickly implements lean tools to eliminate waste and non value-added work
- Teaches lean tools and techniques

"Take apart"   **Kai-zen**   "Make good"

How do you do it?
Planning phase

1. Complete a lean assessment. Use it to identify problems, select a cell or target area, and assemble a core implementation team.

2. Complete a Team Charter with the core implementation team. Ensure that there is a project champion for the kaizen workshop.

3. Bring the Team Charter to upper management for feedback and make any necessary adjustments.

4. Communicate to all workers who will be affected well before the event. Make sure they understand what will happen, when it will happen and what is expected from them.

Kaizen Milestone Worksheet																

Value Stream: Customer A   Date: 2/20   Page 1 of 2
Value Stream Focus: DEMAND

Specific Event	Task	Duration	Person	Weekly Schedule											
				1	2	3	4	5	6	7	8	9	10	11	12
5S	Sort	1 month	D.T.	△	▲										

Kaizen Workshop phase

5. Train the team in lean concepts (4 to 8 hours).

6. Begin the kaizen by applying 5S to the work area.

7. Next, observe the cell or area in action, create a record of present methods (usually through videotaping and photographs), and analyze them. Generate statistics for cycle time, defect rates, etc. Develop a Standard Work Combination Table and Standard Work Chart. (See **Standard Work**)

8. Break the team down into smaller groups to brainstorm and discuss ways to eliminate waste in the work cell. Test the ideas on the work cell and observe their effects.

9. Implement the immediate improvements and develop 30-day follow-up improvements.

10. Measure the results.

11. Report results to the management team and present 30-60-90 day follow-up improvements.

Follow-up phase

12. Continue to implement ideas and monitor results. Monitor the improvements and measure the results. Create standards from improvements.

13. Submit Status Reports on a regular basis. The Status Reports are directed to the champion to communicate the status of the project.

Note: Every area identified as an issue/problem needs a plan for resolution.

14. Make a final report when the project is complete.

This report is often called a Sunset Report. It is completed once the Team Charter has been fulfilled. The Sunset Report will provide a portion of the knowledge attained by this team to be shared by others.

Key Points to Remember

- Kaizen workshops can focus on one activity in one or more areas, for example:
  - Implementing quick changeover on 3 machines
  - Implementing the 5S system in 1 cell, and really focus on those activities, in-depth

Or, a kaizen workshop can focus on one cell and try to implement a number of lean tools in 5 days. For example:
  - Implement the 5S system
  - Implement quick changeover
  - Implement standardized work

- A kaizen workshop can only be successful with strong management support and cooperation from the workforce.
- In kaizens, the Planning phase and the Follow-up phase are just as important as the Workshop phase itself. Unfortunately, they are often neglected, and companies do not get close to the benefit that they could.
- Simple kaizen workshops should be fast: 3 to 5 days or less.
- Complex kaizen events, like a 2-4 week rearrangement of an entire process (10+ machines or stations and 20+ workers), should not be done until at least 5 (preferably 10) simple kaizens have been completed. This assumes the kaizen team is available and are capable of accomplishing a larger kaizen event.

Kanban (Pull System)

Store			Preceding Process
Shelf No.	Item Back No.		
Item No.			
Item Name			
Car Type			Subsequent Process
Box Capacity	Box Type	Issue No.	

Why use it?

The kanban system is used to create a "pull" flow of material or information in a manufacturing operation. Internal kanbans regulate flow within the factory. External kanbans regulate flow from suppliers or from customers.

Who does it?

Lean team with special training in kanbans.

How long will it take to do?

Several weeks for a single multi-station cell.
Approximately 3 to 6 months for a line.

What does it do?

- Kanban is a signal card indicating the need for material.
- It lets the preceding process know when it withdraws a part, allowing it to reproduce or reorder that part.
- Kanban controls the pull system. Product is produced and supplies are ordered *only* when a kanban card says to do so—not to schedule, but when used (i.e., pulled).
- Kanban reduces inventory.

There are three types of kanban:

A **withdrawal kanban** is a printed card indicating the number of parts to be removed from the supermarket and supplied downstream.

A **production kanban** is a printed card indicating the number of parts that need to be processed to replenish what was taken.

A **signal kanban** is a printed card indicating the reorder point has been attained and a particular material lot needs to be replenished.

The Origin of Kanban
Kanban, in Japanese, means "card," "billboard," or "sign." The term is often used synonymously for the card itself and the material flow system developed by the Toyota Production System.

 How do you do it?

1. Kanbans are created after a line has been balanced and designed. It is the last step in the standardization and control of a process. A few rules in particular make the kanban system effective:
   a. Downstream processes withdraw items from upstream processes.
   b. Upstream processes produce only what is withdrawn.
   c. Only 100 percent defect-free products are sent.
   d. Always try to eliminate variation in flow at different processes and operations.
   e. Kanban cards move with the goods to provide visual control.
   f. The number of kanban cards determines the amount of Work-In-Process (WIP) inventory.
   g. Continue to try to reduce the number of kanban cards in circulation to force improvements.
2. A withdrawal kanban is a printed card indicating the number of parts to be removed from the supermarket and supplied downstream. (Normally, 1 kanban per container of parts.)

Store			Preceding Process
Shelf No.	Item Back No.		
Item No.			
Item Name			
Car Type			Subsequent Process
Box Capacity	Box Type	Issue No.	

3. A production kanban is a printed card indicating the number of parts that need to be processed to replenish what was taken.

Store		Process
Shelf No.	Item Back No.	
Item No.		
Item Name		
Car Type		

4. A signal kanban is a printed card indicating the reorder point has been attained and a particular material lot needs to be replenished.

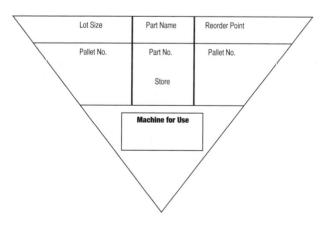

Lot Size	Part Name	Reorder Point
Pallet No.	Part No.	Pallet No.
	Store	
	Machine for Use	

5. To determine the number of kanbans needed at a process, the total amount must cover process lead time. The kanban formula will help you determine how many kanbans are needed.

$$\frac{\text{Process lead time}}{\text{Takt time}} \text{ / quantity of parts per kanban} + X = \begin{array}{c}\text{Number of}\\ \text{kanbans}\\ \text{needed}\end{array}$$

Quantity of parts per kanban is the minimum lot size that can move through the value stream.

X is the safety margin, or management's confidence in the system. X can represent various reasons why a customer order may not be successfully completed (weather, wasted process times, etc.).

Example:
Process lead time = 5 days, totaling 2,300 work minutes in those 5 days
  Takt time = 20 minutes
  Quantity of parts per kanban (or minimum lot size) = 5 units or parts
  X factor = 5

$$\left(\frac{2300}{20} \text{ / } 5\right) + 5 = 28$$

Other Examples:
Kanban manages and controls a pull system.
1. Withdrawal kanbans tell the runner in the process how many units he or she should pull from the finished-goods supermarket and stage in shipping for delivery to the customer.
2. Production kanbans tell operators in the cell how many units must be produced to replenish those pulled from finished goods by the runner.

3. Signal kanbans at the In-process supermarket between machining and the cell tell the operator how many units have been pulled from the supermarket.
4. Signal kanbans just upstream of machining tell the supplier how many units have been pulled from raw material inventory.

Supermarkets: A discussion

Without kanban, supermarkets are merely shelves—just another place to store things. So, when you hear about the lean supermarket system, it also means that kanban is being used!

Finished Goods Supermarket

The supermarket used by shipping is called a "finished goods supermarket." This type of supermarket allows shipping to remove the quantity of product needed when ordered by the customer. This picking, and the replacement that accompanies it, is managed like any supermarket: it is a system where something is not replaced until it is removed.

In-Process Supermarket

Where continuous flow is not possible you can use an In-process supermarket system. A supermarket of work-in-process may be necessary to ensure flow is possible. It is used when multiple demands on a machine or a cell exist.

Toyota found the supermarket to be the best alternative in scheduling those upstream processes that cannot flow continuously. As you improve the flow, the need for supermarkets may decrease. Remember, supermarkets are a compromise to the ideal state, as are pitch and buffer and safety inventory. You will not achieve your ideal state overnight, but must continually work toward that ideal state.

Key Points to Remember

- Kanban is the heart of a pull system. It uses standard containers or lot sizes with a single card attached to each. When the inventory represented by that card is used, the card acts as a signal to indicate that more inventory is needed. In this way inventory is provided only when needed, and only in the amount needed.
- Quality is built in at each process, and processes should never send any defective goods downstream. Passing problems downstream causes confusion and hides the source of problems—and makes it that much longer before you solve them.
- Kanbans always move with the goods to ensure Just-In-Time information and visual control at all times.

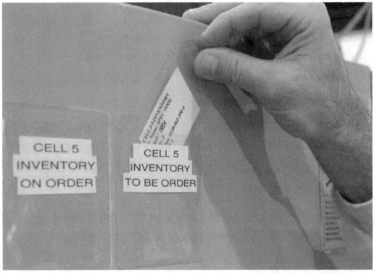

Special type kanbans for consumable or perishable material (i.e., inserts, washers, nuts, bolts, drill bits, etc.) should be placed in an accessible location.

Lean Metrics (OEE)

Why use it?

To be able to identify problems, determine targets, study the impact of improvement activities, check results, and make appropriate adjustments. Lean metrics provide a means, thus helping to drive continuous improvement and waste elimination.

Who does it?

There are two levels: plant wide (or value stream wide) and floor level.

1. A lean team determines plantwide (or value stream) metrics, with the participation of the plant manager and manufacturing manager (if they are not already team members).
2. Operators and other workers help gather data, based on specific measures that might be important to their jobs. This is called stratification.

How long will it take to do?

It takes about a week to perform the initial assessment, select lean metrics, get buy-in, and select targets.

What does it do?

- Assesses performance in accordance with typical lean measures
- Selects the best lean metrics for your situation
- Calculates baseline measures
- Using those baseline measures, selects targets
- Monitors progress

How do you do it?

There are 8 steps in developing and implementing metrics.

The 8 Steps of Metrics

1. Review the Team Charter for strategic direction.
2. Perform a lean manufacturing assessment.
3. Determine the lean metrics.
4. Get management buy-in for the metrics.
5. Calculate baseline measures.
6. Select targets for each metric.
7. Make the metrics visual.
8. Continue to measure and post results.

---

1. Review the Team Charter for strategic direction. (See **Lean Communications**)

2. Perform a lean manufacturing assessment.
Lean metrics are always based on the 7 deadly wastes. To find the metrics that best fit your value stream, you should perform a lean manufacturing assessment. The lean assessment will give you an overall idea of where you are on the lean implementation scale, but it will not provide the day-to-day detail you need to measure progress. For that you need lean metrics.

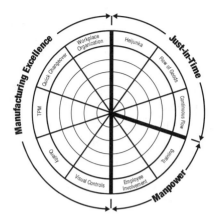

3. Determine the lean metrics.

Determining the metrics that are right for your organization depends a great deal on the circumstances of your situation. However, there is a key set of lean measures.

Key Lean Metrics
• Inventory turns
• Throughput (parts per man-hour)
• First-time-through capability (first-time quality or first-time yield)
• On-time-delivery
• Safety OSHA recordables
• Value-added (percent, per person, per direct labor hour)

Other Lean Metrics
• Personnel turnover
• Equipment use based on customer demand
• Overall equipment effectiveness (OEE—see box, next page)
• Cycle time (order to ship)

Overall Equipment Effectiveness (OEE)

OEE is calculated by multiplying *availability* X *performance efficiency* X *quality rate*. Take one of these components, for example availability. To calculate availability, you need to divide actual operating time by net available time. When you examine operating time more closely you will find that it is heavily influenced by changeover time!

So OEE gives management a tool to monitor an overall value stream or cell, and it gives an operator a tool to improve operating time.

4. Get management buy-in for the metrics.

Use the catchball process between the team and management to reach agreement on the metrics to be utilized. (In catchball, the team members and managers "toss" ideas and proposals back and forth refining them until a consensus is achieved.)

5. Calculate baseline measures.

Measure each metric to determine your starting point. Also decide:
a. Who will be responsible for doing the measurement
b. How often measured
c. The form used to gather the data
d. To whom the data will be reported
e. The type of graph it will be displayed in, and where

6. Select targets for each metric.

Don't forget to play catchball again.

7. Make the metrics visual.

• Measures that are not displayed visually *will fail*!
• Practice "information democracy." Post measures for all to see. Metrics should do only one thing: provide information, because information that is not shared becomes useless.
• Visual posting also creates buy-in.

8. Continue to measure and post results.

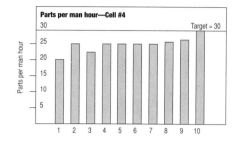

Key Points to Remember

- After determining the lean metrics that will achieve the targets the team has established, it is important to initiate a round of catchball with upper management. The purpose is to ensure their commitment to the metrics.

- Lean metrics should be easily stratified, so that they provide a total measure for the entire value stream as well as specific measures for individual cells—and real improvement. A good example is Overall Equipment Effectiveness (OEE).

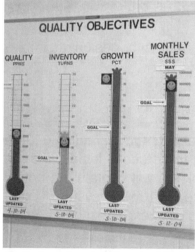

Each department, cell, and administrative area should have measures visible.

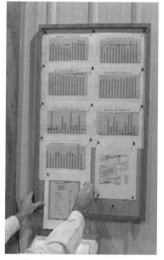

Posted measurements should be kept current!

Lean Office (Paper File System) NEW!

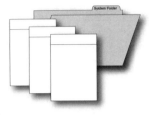

Why use it?

To ensure paperwork is organized and processed correctly. This is an integral part of an organization's paper system. It can assist work flow in quality, finance, billing, planning, etc. Any department can benefit from using all, or parts of, what is contained in this section.

Who does it?

The Lean project team will work to create the file system with input from employees. Everyone will eventually be required to follow the new paper file system standards.

How long will it take to do?

This will require regular, ongoing meetings for designing, implementing, and maintaining.

What does it do?

The paper system will consist of creating and maintaining three types of folders: the system folder, the process folder, and the reference folder. Each of these folders will contain the actual process work or information required to run the system. Later in this section each of these folders will be addressed in detail.

How do you do it?

There is a 3 step procedure for this section. The steps are:

1. Create the system folder.
2. Create the process folder (or kanban) and reference folder.
3. Establish a holding point.

1. Create the system folder.

The system folder will be the "headquarters" of all pertinent information about the processes or value streams. It is the organized listing (i.e., processes) of the work for the entire lean system. The system folder will:

• Centralize all process information
• Create a visual aid for document control (having a list of all processes in a document within a system folder)
• Assist in obtaining predictable output
• Support continuous improvement
• Allow for process knowledge to be further owned by the organization

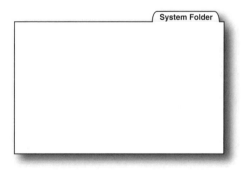

System Folder

A. Inside of system folder

Inside of the system folder will be the "brains" of the entire Lean Office. It will contain the Process Master Document, Process Review Schedule, and the Training Matrix. Other documents may be included to support the overall concept of the system folder.

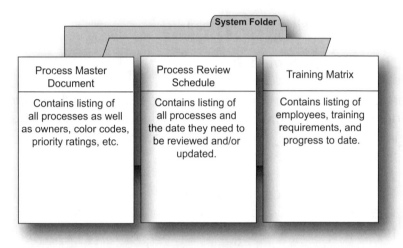

Process Master Document	Process Review Schedule	Training Matrix
Contains listing of all processes as well as owners, color codes, priority ratings, etc.	Contains listing of all processes and the date they need to be reviewed and/or updated.	Contains listing of employees, training requirements, and progress to date.

B. Outside of system folder

The outside of the system folder will have the folder priority rating displayed and the status of the folder. The folder priority rating is a color coded visual aid representing each type of process. A color will be assigned to Critical 1, 2, 3 (multiple colors may be assigned), Non-Critical, and Reference processes.

Critical is defined as those administrative processes that directly impact the financial status of the organization (e.g., entering customer order, invoicing, providing service at point of sale, etc.).

Non-critical is defined as those processes that are necessary but do not have an immediate financial impact on the organization (e.g., performance appraisals, interviews, etc.).

Reference information is defined as information required on an as-needed basis (e.g., auditing manuals, standard operating procedures, environmental guidelines, etc.).

A legend representing the status of the process folder should be displayed on the outside of the folder as a visual aid. A process folder can be in an active or passive state.

An **active state folder** would contain work that needs to be completed and should reside in a horizontal position.

Active State

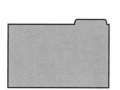

An **passive state folder** would contain work that has already been completed and should reside in a vertical position.

Passive State

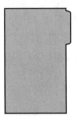

The active or passive state visual cue will accomplish the following:

- Standard communications as to what work is being performed and what is not
- Identification to the manager/supervisor/coach when work is piling up
- Identification of when work has been completed

The system folder should always remain in the active state. The process folder will start out in the active state. It will be moved to a passive state once the work is completed.

The active and passive state should be graphically displayed on the outside of the folder.

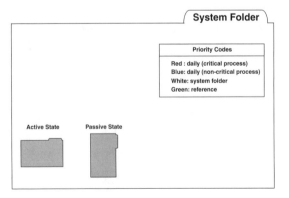

C. Process Master Document

The administrative processes need to be identified before the process folder is created. This will be accomplished by the creation of the Process Master Document. The Process Master Document contains a listing of all the processes required to meet a customer demand.

The Process Master Document as an electronic version should be maintained and secured by the departmental manager. The hardcopy will be contained in the System Folder.

The six steps to creating the Process Master Document are:

1. Prioritization and classification of processes
2. Identification of process owners (process owners are those individuals who can perform that process at an expertise level and will maintain the standard in practice and in writing)
3. Determination of color codes (color codes are a visual aid to communicate the priority level of a process)
4. Creation of process flowcharts (See **Value Stream Mapping**)
5. Validation of the processes (verification the process is currently being run the best way)
6. Train staff of the process(es)

Remember, these are guidelines and the team should discuss what will work best given the requirements of the organization.

2. Create the process folder (or kanban) and reference folder.

Using all process names collected from Step 1, a separate folder for each process will be created. (These will be referred to as process folders, work kanbans, or simply kanbans.)

There are 3 parts to the process folder:

1. The actual work
2. Process Flowchart or Standard Work (See **Standard Work**)
3. Volume capture, which is to identify the cycle time that a process requires (See Value-Added Time Reporting Log later in this section)

A process folder is located at point-of-use. It is the working document required to ensure that the process steps are done in a consistent manner, to the standards set forth by the owner of that process (which follows organizational policy). The information contained in the folder will contribute dramatically to reducing work variation through following a standard. This improves work quality.

A process folder is the "keeper" of all working knowledge required to complete that process. It will also contain the actual work required by the customer (i.e., another department, vendor, etc.). Each process listed in the Process Master Document must have its own process folder.

A process folder will:

- Detail all tasks necessary to complete the process
- Serve as a visual tool to ensure consistent work is accomplished
- Support continuous improvement
- Allow process knowledge to be further owned by the organization

A. Inside of process folder

The process folder will contain the Value-Added Time Reporting Log, Process Flowchart, and the Work Unit that must be completed. Remember, the folder is a "kanban." It is a signal to do work. Later is this chapter you will determine how much work should be placed in each folder.

The Process Flowchart should be placed as the first document within the process folder. It is recommended that the flowchart reside in a clear document sleeve for ease of retrieval so improvement ideas can be documented.

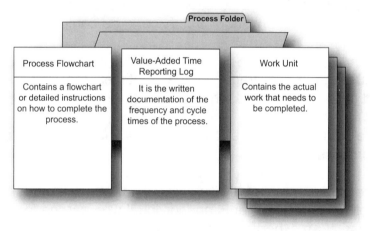

B. Outside of process folder

The outside of the process folder will be labeled in two locations: a label placed on the front of the folder and the other on the tab identifying the process.

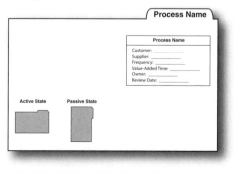

The labeling will be used as a visual aid for quick retrieval of the folder. It also contributes towards eliminating the waste of waiting.

The following information should be standard on every folder:

Process Name: the name of the process as it is listed on the Process Master Document

Supplier: the most upstream process supplying work requirements for the department or value stream

Customer: the most downstream name of the department or process requesting work or a service to be completed or provided

Frequency: the average number of times the process will need to be completed each day, week, or month

Value-Added Time: the total cycle time needed to complete the process

Owner: the name of the individual to whom ownership is established. The owner is an individual who can perform that process at an expertise level and will maintain the standard in practice and in writing.

Review Date: the date the process must be reviewed for improvements and/or revisions

This information should be affixed to each folder. Initially, create a few process folders and then gradually add more as experience is gained.

C. Value-Added Time Reporting Log

The Value-Added Time Reporting Log will be utilized to track the process cycle times. This will be ongoing throughout the Lean project. The Log will be forwarded to the manager monthly for further analysis and record keeping. It will provide:

- An accurate, data driven departmental performance indicator
- A current analysis of work loads
- A way to look for continuous improvement ideas
- Data to justify assistance when work volume increases

The Log should be filled out every time a process is started and ended, along with who completed the work. The Log should be placed on the inside front flap of the process folder.

Value-Added Time Reporting Log

Name _____ Date _____

Department _____ Job Title or Function _____

Process Name	Date	Start Time	End Time	Initials	Comments

D. Process Flowchart

A process flowchart is a visual representation of a sequence of activities or tasks needed to complete a process. It can be represented by using icons. (See **Problem Solving Methodology**)

Note: Detailed written instructions can also suffice for this step.

3. Establish a holding point.

It is important to create a physical device and place the organizational knowledge (process folders) in a common location.

Note: As you begin to create and collect information about the processes, immediately begin to place the process folders in a common device at a specific location. All of the processes cannot be done at once. The ones that are initially targeted are to be placed in a common area. The process folder will start out in an active state because it contains work that needs to be completed. The process folders should be placed as close to point-of-use as possible.

Key Points to Remember

- Start with a good representation of the processes; you will not be able to work on all of them at once.
- Gain a consensus on the critical processes, as they should be the first process folders created.
- Keep the color code simple at first. Do not try to complicate this or you might lose enthusiasm.
- Always work to communicate the need of this system. Emphasize how it will assist in reducing stress by having defined processes and clear standards.
- Continue to recognize the team in their efforts.
- The folder system (and leveling) is critical in obtaining continuous flow for paperwork; take it one step at a time.

The paper file system should be flexible to meet the changing needs of the organization. Ensure everyone is trained in how the system works.

Modifications of the paper file system can be applied to individual office areas.

Lean Communications

Team Charter
-
-
-
-
-

Why use it?

To effectively ensure that lean teams utilize effective planning and reporting communication tools in their lean project. It will require using the Team Charter, Meeting Information Form, Status Report, and Sunset Report.

Who does it?

1. The team leader is responsible for the various communication tools.

2. The lean team is responsible for contributing and following the meeting procedures.

How long will it take to do?

The Team Charter and Sunset Reprot takes about 1 hour each to create.

The Meeting Information Form and Status Report takes about 15 minutes per week.

What does it do?

- Standardizes communication
- Ensures strategic alignment
- Ensures team discipline

How do you do it?
The Team Charter

The Team Charter is to be completed by the core team assigned to the specific lean project. The Team Charter has the following attributes:

1. Completing a Team Charter is the first important step in any lean project. Ensure everyone is on the same page in reference to the team's mission/scope and deliverables.

2. It is a living document and will change as conditions occur. It should be updated and posted in a common area.

3. The Team Charter will list the deliverables appropriate to the project.

4. Do not commit to something that is not realistic. Gain a consensus on the Team Charter from the team.

5. The champion of the team must ensure that proper resources are committed. The champion usually does not attend all meetings but is available to remove roadblocks, commit necessary resources, provide encouragement, and break down departmental barriers.

6. The team leader is responsible for the day-to-day or week-to-week activities. He or she will schedule meetings and inform the champion of problems and progress to date.

7. The champion should review the Team Charter and agree to it prior to committing any resources.

TEAM CHARTER

Mission—Charter:
• What the team is to do.
• How will the team complete its mission?

Deliverables:

Expected Scope/Approach/Activities:

Strategic Alignment Factors:

Timeframe/Duration:

Team Resources:

Role	Name(s)	Participation Level	Skills Required
Team Leader(s)			•
Core Team Members			•
Extended Team Members			•
Team Facilitator			•
Administrative Support			•
Team Champion			•
Steering Body Members			•

Team Process:

Process Item	Frequency	Audience/Distribbution, Day(s)/Time(s)
Information Distribution	After Meetings	Team members, Team champion
Team Meetings		
Status Reporting		

Key Customers and Suppliers:

Company Name (Ext.) Functional Area (Int.)	Relationship		Level			Reviewer(s) Names
	Customer	Supplier	Economic	Operational	User/Tech	
Internal						
Customer Service						
Engineering						
Information Tech.						
Manufacturing						
Marketing						
Purchasing						
Quality						

Assumptions:

Risks:

Internal Issues:

External Issues:

Meeting Information Form

The Meeting Information Form provides the team with a structured approach to effective meetings, including detailed agendas and action items. The importance of this cannot be underestimated. Listed below are some basic principles that should be followed in regards to this form:

1. Everyone at the meeting must be made aware of the agenda times and topics.

2. Action items/due dates are assigned and reviewed. Every attempt is made to adhere to these.

3. Project milestones are met to ensure lean project completion.

Meeting Information Form

Meeting:

Date:
Time:
Place:

Purpose:

Contents
- ☒ **Distribution**
- ☒ **Agenda**
- ☒ **Minutes**
- ☒ **Action Items**

DISTRIBUTION

Participants		Roles		FYI (Copies to)

AGENDA

Time	Item	Who	Duration

Additional Information

MINUTES

Summary	

Issues	Agreements Reached
1.	
2.	

Discussion Notes

Attachments

Next Meeting

Date:	Time:	Place:

ACTION ITEMS

No.	Action Item	Assigned to	Opened	Due	Status
1					
2					
3					
4					

Status Report

The Status Report is directed to the champion to communicate the status of the project.

Note: Every area identified as a Concern (Issues) needs a Plan for resolution. This will give the champion confidence that the team has control of the project.

STATUS REPORT

Team Name:

Date:

Status:
• Are you on time?

Accomplishments:
• What are the main accomplishments of the team to date?

Concerns (Issues):
• Areas that problems may have been encountered or ahead or behind schedule to milestones

Plans (How to Resolve Issues):
• Plan for the team to address what was listed in the Concerns (Issues) area

Forward to Team Champion/Owner/CEO

Project Manager/Team Leader: "Confidential"
Phone/email:

Sunset Report

The Sunset Report provides a summation of the knowledge attained by the team and is to be shared with others. It is completed once the Team Charter has been fulfilled. The team leader typically completes the Sunset Report.

SUNSET REPORT

Program Name _____

Team: **Date:**

Executive Summary
- Charter
  -   —
  -   —

- **Expected Deliverables**
  -   —

Recommendations to Management
- Topic
  - — Recommendations
  - — Benefits

Recommendations to Others
- Topic
  - — Recommendations
  - — Benefits

Accomplishments
-
-
-

Issues
-
-
-

Plans
-
-
-

Lessons Learned
- What Worked
  -   —
  -   —

- What Didn't Work
  -   —
  -   —

Summary
-
-

Team Leader Info:
-

Key Points to Remember

- It has often proved helpful to have the Team Charter semi-completed prior to the first lean team meeting. This may save some time in presenting the core information.
- The Team Charter is a living document and should reflect the team's input as it is periodically reviewed.
- The team leader should always prepare an agenda for a meeting. If a kaizen event is going to consume more than a few hours, the team should detail the timetable as much as possible.
- The Meeting Information Form can be quickly completed and distributed to all necessary parties. It is a clear and precise form of communication that ensures everyone is aware of the team's efforts.
- As action items are reviewed, and if necessary deferred, make time in the agenda to review outstanding action items and determine why progress is not occurring in some areas. The team leader should be very responsive to these issues.
- The Sunset Report should be kept in a central location or database for ease of reference by others that may undertake similar projects.
- Keep the time frame for the project to less than 90 days to avoid "project burnout" and "scope creep."

See www.theleanstore.com for these forms in an electronic format.

Line Balancing

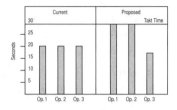

Why use it?

To determine how to best distribute work elements across operators within a work area to meet takt time.

Who does it?

A cross-functional lean team.

How long will it take to do?

Approximately one week or less depending on the complexity of the value stream.

What does it do?

- Evenly loads all workers to the work cells
- Obtains individual cycle time for each operation
- Defines the order in which work elements should be done
- Defines the number of workers needed
- Helps you create a future-state map

How do you do it?

Line balancing is a 6-step process:

1. Choose a process or work area.

2. Obtain individual cycle times for each work element.

3. Add the individual cycle times to obtain the total cycle time.

4. Create the Operator Balance Chart of the current state.

5. Determine the ideal number of operators.

6. Create the Operator Balance Chart of the future state. Evenly distribute the work elements among workers.

Each step now will be explained more in depth.

1. Choose a process or work area.

Be very clear about identifying the process, its beginning and end, and its external customers. (This also applies if you are using value stream management—be accurate and explicit about the parameters of the value stream.)

2. Obtain individual cycle times for each work element.

Obtain individual cycle times for each operation by adding all tasks in an individual operation. Usually a Cycle Time Worksheet is utilized.

Cycle Time Worksheet—Common Attributes

1. Lists all the work elements.

2. Each element is timed for 10 cycles, *on the floor*. **Note:** Do one element at a time (all shifts).

3. For each element, select the following from the data:
   • High time element
   • Low repeatable time element
   • Most frequent time element

4. Total each column to calculate total cycle time.

5. Use most frequent time as the baseline

6. Use low repeatable time as a realistic target. Operator did something different during those cycles. What was it?

7. Use high time to find what occurred during that cycle to cause such a spike.

Example:

Operator 1			Operator 2			Operator 3		
Elmt.	**Desc.**	**Time**	**Elmt.**	**Desc.**	**Time**	**Elmt.**	**Desc.**	**Time**
1	Cut	9.2	1	Pin	7.2	1	Pack	3.9
2	Bore	5.1	2	Key	6.9	2	#2 Pin	6.8
3	Tube	4.3	3	Link	5.1	3	De-burr	5.7
4	Clip	3.8						

Total time 22.4 sec. Total time 19.2 sec. Total time 16.4 sec.

3. Add the individual cycle times to obtain the total cycle time.

Example

Operator 1: cycle time = 22.4 sec.

Operator 2: cycle time = 19.2 sec.

Operator 3: cycle time = 16.4 sec.

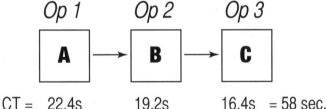

Op 1   Op 2   Op 3

A → B → C

CT = 22.4s   19.2s   16.4s = 58 sec.

total cycle tim e

4. Create the Operator Balance Chart of the current state.
To create a Operator Balance Chart of the current state, (see next page) review the information gathered from all Cycle Time Work Sheets, including cycle times and number of operators for each operation.

Current State Operator Balance Chart

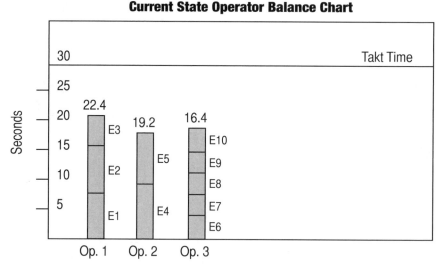

Example:
The bar chart above represents the three operations (Op1, Op2, and Op3) with a takt time of 30 seconds and a total cycle time of 58.3 seconds. (See the preceding information for details for each operation.)

5. Determine the ideal number of operators.
Determine the number of operators needed by dividing total cycle time by takt time. For this example, the calculation is as follows:

Example:

$$\frac{58 \text{ seconds (total cycle time)}}{30 \text{ seconds (takt time)}} = 1.93 \text{ operators}$$

6. Create the Operator Balance Chart of the future state.
Evenly distribute the work elements among workers.

Finally, you must determine how to produce your product with the new number of operators. Create a Operator Balance Chart of the future (or proposed) state.

Operator Balance Chart—Current and Proposed

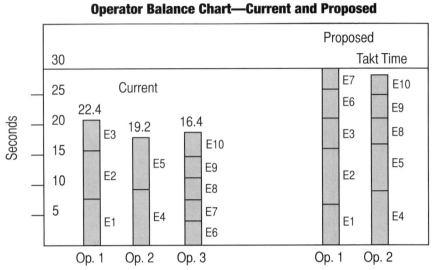

Example:

The need to deploy 1.93 operators presents you with an obvious problem. It means that there is not enough work to occupy worker #3, but you are still paying for that time. This number also provides you with an opportunity to set an improvement target—to eliminate enough waste in the line so that only 2 operators are needed. (The 3rd operator will be utilized elsewhere in the lean value stream.)

A progressively lean process might solve this problem by absorbing operation C into operations A and B, as shown on the Operator Balance Chart Proposed State (future state), but there could be other solutions. An ideal situation is to have every operator working to takt time.

Key Points to Remember

- Set the low repeatable time element as the target.
- Involve workers in timing.
- The Operator Balance Chart can be used to drive kaizen improvements by configuring work elements using magnetic strips to match low repeatable length rather than most frequent length.

Mistake-Proofing (Poka-Yoke)

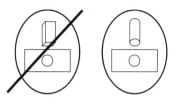

Why use it?

To design error prevention into a product or process to achieve zero defects.

Who does it?

Experienced kaizen teams (requires special training and experience in poka-yoke).

How long will it take to do?

• Simple single workstation: 2 to 4 weeks
• Multiple workstation cell: 6 months
• Entire assembly line: years

What does it do?

• Assures quality in workstation
• Corrects conditions in the process that allow errors
• Supports knowledgeable workers
• Eliminates the potential for operator error

How do you do it?

The aim of mistake-proofing is to become a "Level 5" plant. (See next page.) What level is your plant at now?

There are five levels to mistake-proofing:

1. Paradigm shift
2. Analysis
3. Standardized work
4. Red flag conditions
5. Mistake-proofing devices

Levels of Plant Quality Assurance

Level		Effect	Inspection	Zero Defect Action
1	Plant ships defective products	Many defects and many customer complaints	Judgment inspection	Shut down the factory
2	Plant does not ship defective products	Many defects but few customer complaints	None	Use more inspectors
3	Plant is now reducing defects	Defects produced in one production run are not repeated in future runs	Information feedback inspection; SPC	Boosting engineering-type improvement s
4	Plant processes do not send defects downstream	When defects are produced, they do not get passed on to the next process	Independent inspection by operators using successive self-checks	Training operators to identify and remove defects
5	Plant processes do not create defects	When an error occurs, the process does not produce defects	Process does not allow errors, so no inspection necessary	

1. Paradigm shift

Errors can be prevented! Begin looking for the source of defects, not just the defects themselves, and for opportunities to eliminate them at their source. Everyone must understand that they are playing by a new set of rules. Inspection alone can never achieve zero defects!

Look for the *source* of defects (the root cause), not just the defects themselves. Eliminate root causes at the source. The root cause for defects is in the work process, not the people!

2. Analysis

To analyze the problem you must be able to identify and describe the defect in depth, including the rate of the defect over time. In addition, you need to know exactly where the source of the defect is. Below is an example of a form often used in this analysis.

Mistake-Proofing Analysis Form

Part #	Defect	Rework/ Scrap	Where Found?	Source?	Time-Distance
What is the product?	What is the defect?	What was resulting rework or scrap?	Where was defect found?	Where was defect made?	Time between made and found?

Defects and errors are not the same. Defects are the results. Errors are the causes of the results.

Defects vs. Errors

To be a **defect**:
- The part or product must have deviated from specifications
- The part or product does not meet the customer (internal or external) expectations

To be an **error**:
- Something must have deviated from an intended process
- All defects are created by errors, but not all errors result in defects

3. Standardized work

Detail current standardized work and work to eliminate any deviations from that standard. If errors remain, apply problem solving to determine the root cause. Apply mistake-proofing (poka-yoke) to the root cause.

4. Red flag conditions

Identify red flag conditions, which are conditions in the process that commonly allow errors. Red flags are potential root causes of errors.

Red Flag Conditions	
Adjustments	Symmetry
Tooling changes	Asymmetry
Specifications not met	Rapid repetition
Many parts/mixed parts	High volume
Multiple steps	Environmental conditions:
Infrequent production	• Poor lighting
Lack of standards	• Foreign matter
Ineffective standards	• Poor housekeeping

In any operation, the essential ingredient is people. Yet people make errors, which lead to defects. No matter how we strive to avoid errors, sooner or later they will occur. While we tend to accept errors as something natural, we find fault with the people who made them. We try to "fix" the person rather than focusing on the source of errors within the manufacturing environment. Any kind of error that people make can be prevented. People will tend to make fewer errors if their production system is based on the principle that errors can be prevented and regards people as the source of the solutions, not the cause of the error. So look at the process, not the people.

5. Mistake-proofing devices

There are 3 levels of control that error-proofing devices can achieve:

- **Level 1:** Eliminates the error at the source before it occurs
- **Level 2:** Detects the error as it occurs and before it results in a defect
- **Level 3:** Detects the defect after it has been made, but before it reaches the next operation

When you create your device you will need to decide the level that is possible and most appropriate for the situation. Clearly Level 1 is the one that is most desirable, but not always possible or cost effective.

Use the following criteria:

- Is it cost effective?
- Is it simple and easy to implement?
- Is it specifically focused on the problem at hand?
- Is a cross-functional team developing it?

Mistake-proofing devices generally fall into 3 categories:

1. Display devices that provide a visual or auditory alarm that alerts the worker that an error has been made.

2. Jig devices are fixtures that prevent the use of wrong parts or the improper positioning of correct parts. These can be automated to prevent the operation of the machine by using proximity or limit switches.

3. Automatic devices automatically detect errors and stop or prevent further cycle or release of part.

Here are some particular devices worth considering:

- A jig that will not allow wrong parts or that prevents the wrong alignment of parts.
- Detection devices that will not allow a machine to start if a part is missing or out of place (e.g., proximity switch, electronic eye, light curtain).

- Detection devices that will not allow the next step in a process to occur if the previous steps have not been properly completed in the proper sequence (e.g., timers, sequence logic in control, limit switches, torque-controlled devices).
- Devices that automatically adjust part or position so that manual placement/adjustment (which often introduces errors) is not required (e.g., tapered locating pins, parts pushers, locating clamps).
- Devices that inspect previous process to assure that it is properly completed before allowing part to proceed downstream (e.g., power clamps tied to detection device, automatic inspection station between process steps using signal lights, proximity or limit switches utilized for inspection).

Key Points to Remember

- The goal of mistake-proofing is zero defects.
- Never pass a defective product downstream! By eliminating rework and, more importantly, after-sales repairs, you can save a great deal of money, retain your loyal customer base, and add new customers.
- All operators must understand the principles of mistake-proofing and believe that *any error can be prevented* in order to effectively participate in mistake-proofing activities.
- Mistake-proofing reduces cycle time and prevents wastes such as waiting, transport, inspection and, of course, defects.
- Look at the process, not the people, for the root cause of a mistake.
- Machines (manual or robotic) that have been designed to include error-proofing devices assure that the end product will be defect free. (Work teams can participate in the design and improvement of parts processing and assembly operations in order to help prevent defects from occurring.)

Origins of Lean

 Why use it?
To effectively communicate the evolution of lean concepts and tools.

Who does it?
All workers, who will gain an understanding of the origins of lean concepts and practices. This in turn assures that workers comprehend the full value of lean implementations.

How long will it take to do?
Up to 30 minutes.

What does it do?
- Communicates that lean has global origins
- Allows for a broader understanding of lean concepts and tools
- Provides for a solid foundation on which to build a lean system utilizing common nomenclature

 How do you do it?
1. Schedule a time to cover this material at a shift start, monthly meeting, or at the beginning of the team's project.
2. Review briefly the concepts and tools and how they originated from global sources.

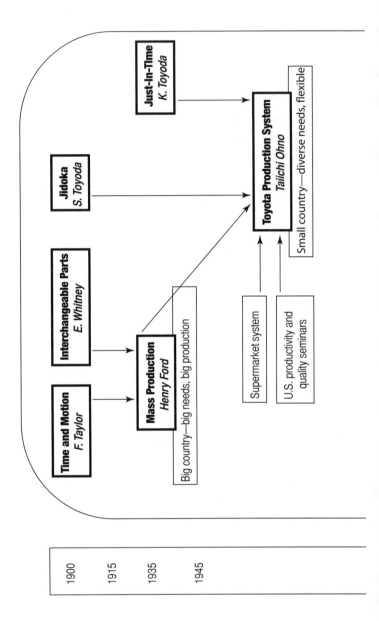

Time and Motion *F. Taylor*	**Interchangeable Parts** *E. Whitney*	**Jidoka** *S. Toyoda*	**Just-In-Time** *K. Toyoda*

Mass Production *Henry Ford*

Big country—big needs, big production

Toyota Production System *Taiichi Ohno*

Small country—diverse needs, flexible

Supermarket system

U.S. productivity and quality seminars

1900
1915
1935
1945

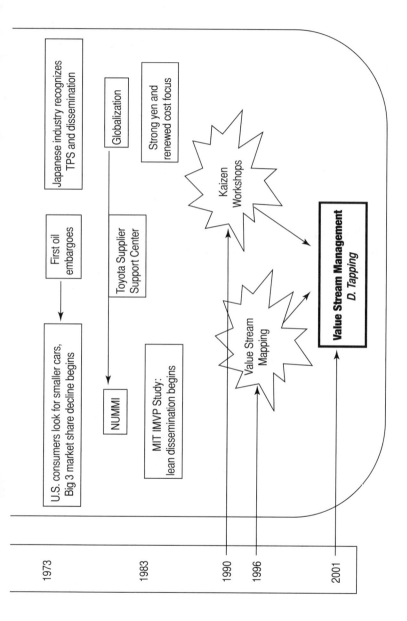

1973	U.S. consumers look for smaller cars, Big 3 market share decline begins
	First oil embargoes
	Japanese industry recognizes TPS and dissemination
1983	NUMMI
	Toyota Supplier Support Center
	Globalization
	Strong yen and renewed cost focus
1990	MIT IMVP Study: lean dissemination begins
1996	Value Stream Mapping
	Kaizen Workshops
2001	**Value Stream Management** *D. Tapping*

- Henry Ford's conveyor system in the 1930s, in conjunction with Japanese market, economic and industrial circumstances, forced Toyota to develop original ways of implementing Ford's ideas (kaizen is born). Toyota could not mass-produce on a level to compete with the United States, so it had to develop large production efficiencies with small volumes of production (it being a small country with diverse products).
- Taiichi Ohno traveled to America in the 1950s and toured its automobile plants. He came away with the supermarket concept (customers in a grocery store expect to have what they need, when they need it, and a kanban card is used to signal replenishment). He later transformed this into the supermarket pull system to support the Just-In-Time philosophy.
- Toyota developed a cost-reduction philosophy. Market conditions (the constant in the equation) set the selling price. Cost and profit became variables. Focusing on internal costs became a philosophical approach and led the drive in improvement initiatives.

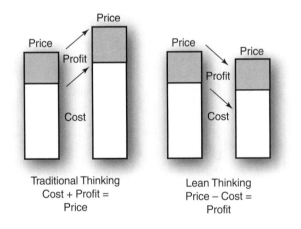

Traditional Thinking
Cost + Profit =
Price

Lean Thinking
Price − Cost =
Profit

- The Toyota Production System (TPS) became global in the 1970s due to of the oil crisis. Toyota's proven flexibility and its internal cost-reduction philosophy and methodology expanded its global presence.
- The Toyota Supplier Support Center was created to foster Toyota's work with U.S. suppliers to implement lean.
- Kaizen workshops and value stream mapping became a craze throughout manufacturing organizations, with limited success.
- The value stream management process begins and is used as the plan for systematic lean implementation. The process allows for kaizen workshops and value stream mapping to be integrated in such a way that lean is sustained.
- It took Toyota 50 years to become world-class. The United States has been at it for 15 to 20 years and is just now beginning to understand it fully.
- TPS is still evolving.

Origins of lean

The Toyota Production System (TPS) is used synonymously with "lean manufacturing" throughout the world. Lean is a compilation of world-class practices adapted from the United States, Germany, and Japan. Today in Japan they refer to Just-In-Time as JIT—an American acronym. Similarly, takt, a German word, refers to "beat" or "rhythm."

The important point is to understand that lean had a global birth; practitioners need not get caught up in whether a particular word or phrase is American, German, or Japanese. The goal is to use the correct concept/tool/technique to improve quality, cost, and delivery in a waste-free environment.

The purpose of lean practices is to eliminate all waste or non value-added activities from a process. The continued focus on the elimination of waste should be a daily, hourly and/or minute-by-minute review. Lean is not meant to eliminate people, but to use them wisely. With that thought in mind, work elements or job duties may need to be modified to accommodate the waste-free environment. This will allow companies to remain globally competitive, with a cross-trained workforce within a safe manufacturing environment.

 Key Points to Remember

- Lean is a journey, not a single event.
- Lean implementation is a process of incremental improvements, and a culture within an organization that supports employee's ideas and involvement.
- Lean will work in any type of organization or industry, but you must be flexible in applying its concepts and tools.
- Continue to benchmark lean organizations: it always helps to "see" lean in action as you progress.

Paced Withdrawal

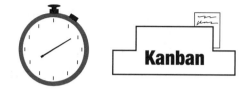

Why use it?

If very repeatable cycle times and common parts are present, paced withdrawal may be used.

Who does it?

A cross-functional lean team or kaizen team, including the workers and managers most directly impacted by the changes.

How long will it take to do?

- 1 day to run through calculations of takt time and pitch
- 1 week to implement in a simple 3 - 4 station operation

What does it do?

- Levels production in a value stream by moving small batches of material through the value stream over time intervals equal to the pitch (See **Pitch**)
- Reduces inventory levels
- Paced withdrawal balances the pace of production against the pace of sales and evenly distributes production over a day or shift

How do you do it?

1. Calculate takt time and pitch.
2. Determine pack-out quantity. Pack-out quantity can be dictated by the customer. If it is not, it can be determined by shipping container size, logical transportable quantity inside the factory, constraints of conveyors moving material, equipment capacity, or by an experienced kaizen team with knowledge of the operation.
3. Create the paced withdrawal, based on customer demand. For example, your paced withdrawal might be 1 box of 32 hammers every 15 minutes. This is your pitch.
4-7. Negotiate with your suppliers regarding delivery frequencies, quantities, and other requirements (container size, durability, etc.).
8. Standardize work.

Example: Electric motors, assembled, and packed

Customer's request: 30 units per skid (pack-out quantity)
Box quantity: 30 units
Maximum capacity of lift truck: 30 units

1. Takt time = 60 seconds

$$\textbf{Takt time} = \frac{28{,}800 \text{ sec. (\# sec. per shift)}}{480 \text{ units (customer requirements per shift)}} = 60 \text{ sec. takt time}$$

2. Pack-out quantity = 30 units

3. Pitch (the time required to produce the pack-out quantity) = 30 minutes

$$\textbf{Pitch} = \frac{60 \text{ sec. (takt time) X } 30 \text{ units (pack-out quantity)}}{60 \text{ seconds}} = 30 \text{ minutes}$$

THE NEW LEAN POCKET GUIDE XL

4. Therefore, you withdraw product every 30 minutes/30 units. Or withdrawing at the customer required pace of 30 minutes.

5. Verify paced shipping.

   a. The customer wants one skid of 30 units every 30 minutes.

   b. Production stops during lunch (12:00-12:30), so that has to become part of the sequence.

   c. The workday lasts from 8:00 am to 4:30 pm.

   d. That gives the appropriate number of pitch sequences (16) to produce the total demand of 480 units (480 units/30 minutes = 16 pack-out withdrawals).

8:00 am packout withdrawal-1	12:30 pm packout withdrawal-9
8:30 am packout withdrawal-2	1:00 pm packout withdrawal-10
9:00 am packout withdrawal-3	1:30 pm packout withdrawal-11
9:30 am packout withdrawal-4	2:00 pm packout withdrawal-12
10:00 am packout withdrawal-5	2:30 pm packout withdrawal-13
10:30 am packout withdrawal-6	3:00 pm packout withdrawal-14
11:00 am packout withdrawal-7	3:30 pm packout withdrawal-15
11:30 am packout withdrawal-8	4:00 pm packout withdrawal-16
Lunch	4:30 pm end of shift

6. Implement paced withdrawal/timed delivery of components in the factory.
    a. Withdraw large or significant components from supermarket in pack-out quantities and deliver to workstations at pitch intervals.
    b. Small or low-value components should be delivered in larger quantities at less frequent intervals.
7. Lay out withdrawal and delivery routes.
8. Create standardized work for withdrawal and delivery route workers.

Key Points to Remember

- Paced withdrawal is used when demand is expected to be even—when the pack-out quantity is constant. (When you have variations in pack-out quantities, the more effective tool is heijunka.)
- If you do not meet demand *on time,* three things should happen:
    1. Immediately notify management.
    2. Use buffer or safety stock to fill the order.
    3. Fix the problem.
- Paced withdrawal is used when you have no product variety in the value stream.
- As you gain the ability to decrease batch sizes, you may negotiate with your customer for smaller and more frequent deliveries.
- Paced withdrawal is a system of inventory control. Customers usually want products in containers that hold a standard pack-out quantity. Paced withdrawal levels production by dividing the total requirement for a shift or day into batches equal to that pack-out quantity.

The concept of paced withdrawal can also apply to kitting. Kitting is the packaging and delivering of the components required for the cell to make the part at a certain time.

Packed withdrawal will help to eliminate the need for excess inventory. Create "mailboxes" for only the tooling required.

Perishable Tool Management

Why use it?

To introduce and utilize a structured, proactive system to manage perishable tools.

Who does it?

The program should be initiated and driven by an operations or production manager with the help of a cross-functional team of operators and maintenance workers.

How long will it take to do?

6 to 8 weeks initially; ongoing as it is implemented plantwide.

What does it do?

- Maximizes tooling life, which reduces tool cost
- Reduces defects caused by worn or broken tools
- Reduces unplanned downtime due to tool breakage
- Reduces tool inventories
- Technologically improves tooling from the supplier, due to the sharing of information (tool life, history, etc.)

How do you do it?

The perishable tool management system has five steps:

1. Generate the strategy.
2. Change tooling pro-actively.
3. Manage old tooling.
4. Request new tooling when needed.
5. Deliver and set up new tooling.

A brief explanation of each step follows.

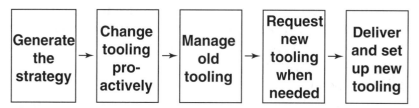

| Generate the strategy | → | Change tooling pro-actively | → | Manage old tooling | → | Request new tooling when needed | → | Deliver and set up new tooling |

1. Generate the strategy.

   a. Identify one specific tool (boring bar, OD rougher, groove tool, etc.) for the first machine you wish to implement tool life management.
   b. Track the number of parts it takes for this tool to wear out or break (must track like material).
   c. Once established, set that number as the benchmark.
   d. Change the given tool when the benchmark number has been reached.
   e. Repeat with all tools used on the given machine.
   f. Begin implementing plantwide by repeating on all machines.
   g. Select a cell with long-run production jobs, if possible, as the first cell to implement the system.

2. Change tooling pro-actively.

   a. Perishable tooling should be changed pro-actively, before it comes to the end of its life and causes defects, abnormalities, or downtime.
   b. Whenever possible, a machine monitoring system should be part of the strategy that counts cycles and knows when it is time for a pro-active tool change.
   c. If possible, a visual control should be in place to indicate when it is time to replace the tool.
   d. If a visual control is not possible, the operators must be able to rely on documentation that will tell them it is time to change the tool, based on machine monitoring system.

3. Manage old tooling.

    a. To manage old tooling, it must be discarded, reviewed, repaired or reworked, recycled, or returned to the vendor.

    b. If tooling is at the end of its life, it should be managed using set procedures.

    c. If the tooling is to be sent back for repair or rework, or recycling to the vendor, it should be placed in a designated area.

4. Request new tooling when needed.

    a. The operator will reorder using the system available in the plant. When a tool has been discarded, a requisition card is used. (See following example)

    b. When a replenishment card-based system is used, the operator places the card in the designated area to request the new tooling. It is sent to the crib or rework area, and the tool is then provided. After tooling is replaced, the card is put back in the designated spot.

    c. Make it pro-active! Timing is everything. The request must be made while the tool is still being used. Then, when it's time to change the tool, a new one is there!

5. Deliver and set up new tooling.

    a. Once the new tool is delivered, it must be set up.

    b. The operator should follow the standard work procedures for this process.

Sample Requisition Card

Tool Number:	Tool Use:
Work Order Number:	Quantity Ordered:
Account Number:	Foreman Code:
Requisition Request By:	Date Request:
Requisition Approved By:	Date Approved:
Requisition Delivered By:	Date Delivered:

Sample Replenishment Card

Market Address   **Number**   **Line Side Address**

Tool Number   **Route**

Tool Description   **Dock**

Comment   **Quantity**   **Serial Number**

Key Points to Remember

- Begin by utilizing your most seasoned machinists in first implementing tool life management.
- Make it policy to change tools at or slightly before the benchmark number.
- Repeat with all tools for all machines plant wide.
- Experiment. Do not be afraid to bump the benchmark number up in small increments in order to get maximum usage from each tool!

Vending type machines are now being used for perishable tooling and plant consumables. This does not replace good, tooling practices. Use whichever system makes the most sense for your value stream needs.

Pitch

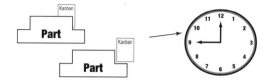

Why use it?

Single-piece lots are rarely economical for material movement between workers or factories (supplier to customer). Pitch is the time element to produce the pack-out quantity for shipping. Pitch is the current best time for the lot size for material shipping and moving material within a plant.

Who does it?

The lean team calculates and determines a reasonable pitch. The pack-out container size influences pitch and may be selected by the customer.

How long will it take to do?

Up to 5 minutes. (You may need to contact the customer to determine their ideal lot size for shipment—that would be the pitch increment.)

What does it do?

When actual takt time is too short to easily pull product through the system you must create an alternate means to pace your flow. Pitch is the adjusted takt time to pull product throughout the value stream when the takt time is too short. Pitch will:

- Set the optimal lot flow size and frequency for material shipping and delivery
- Set the pace for flowing product/parts for the manufacturing organization to maintain continuous flow

- Allow you to respond to problems much faster than in the batch mode
- Improve inventory control

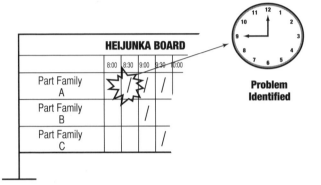

A heijunka board helps you manage your value streams at pitch increments.

Note: Pitch should not be used within a work cell to determine material and movement.

How do you do it?

1. Calculate takt time.
2. Determine pack-out quantity (the shipment quantity required by the customer).
3. Multiply takt time by pack-out quantity and divide by 60 seconds.

   Pitch = takt time X pack-out quantity

Example:

1. Takt time = 60 seconds
2. Pack-out quantity = 30 parts per skid
3. Pitch = 60 seconds (1 minute) takt time X 30 parts per second = 1,800 seconds (divide by 60 seconds) or a 30 minute pitch

Key Points to Remember

- Pack-out quantity determines pitch.
- When the customer does not specify pack-out quantity, it may be dictated by shipping container size.
- Other determinants of pack-out quantity:
  - Logical transportable quantity in factory—create a pitch that makes sense within your organization, considering production volumes and type of part
  - Weight capacity or size of conveyance devices (conveyors, lift trucks, automation)
  - Judgment of kaizen team
- Consider administrative work (i.e., orders, quotes, engineering drawings, invoices, expense reports, employment applications, etc.) for pitch.

Problem Solving Methodology

Why use it?

To create a common language of problem solving concepts and tools, and to provide a systematic approach to continuous improvement.

Who does it?

Everyone, at all levels of an organization, both individuals and groups.

How long will it take to do?

One hour to several weeks depending on the complexity of the issue. The important thing is that the method be followed sequentially.

What does it do?

- Gives the lean team an approach to defining the reason for the problem
- Prevents problems from returning
- Leads towards better standards and a visual factory
- Provides a simple method for people to be involved at all levels
- Provides a common language and approach for solving problems
- If done correctly, has the most potential to solve problems permanently

Note: See the Six Sigma section for a more sophisticated problem solving methodology.

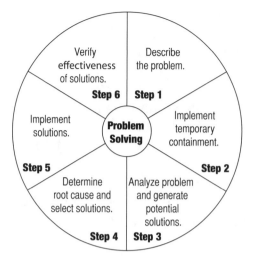

The circle diagram contains:

- Step 1: Describe the problem.
- Step 2: Implement temporary containment.
- Step 3: Analyze problem and generate potential solutions.
- Step 4: Determine root cause and select solutions.
- Step 5: Implement solutions.
- Step 6: Verify effectiveness of solutions.

Center: **Problem Solving**

How do you do it?

This problem solving methodology involves a 6-step method. It has several advantages:

- It is simple
- Both individuals and groups can use it
- It can be used at all levels of an organization
- It provides a common language and approach

6-Step Problem Solving Method

1. Describe the problem.
2. Implement temporary containment.
3. Analyze problem and generate potential solutions.
4. Determine root cause and select solutions.
5. Implement solutions.
6. Verify effectiveness of solutions.

---

1. Describe the problem.

This is the crucial step! Approach it as follows:

a. Write a statement describing the problem. A good problem statement describes a situation both in terms of your own experience and in measurable terms. Understand the basic flow of the work and the bottlenecks.

b. The statement should be:
- Specific—what is it and what is it not? How big of a problem is it?
- Time-bound—when did it first appear?
- Current—what is the present trend of the problem? Is it increasing, decreasing, or unchanging?

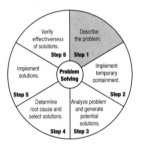

2. Implement temporary containment.

a. How can the customer (internal or external) be protected from this problem (additional inspection, additional operations, etc.)?

b. Implement the appropriate protection method (this is temporary containment).

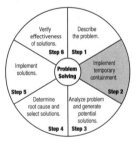

3. Analyze problem and generate potential solutions.

Now that a problem has been identified, it is time to analyze the problem carefully.

a. Gather data on the problem.

b. Use analysis tools to identify at least 3 potential causes. If possible, use benchmarking to discover solutions; ask if best practices can be used. (If you can generate only one potential cause, it is likely that you have found the problem's true root cause.)

c. Split off additional problems you find. (Frequently, during the analysis phase, what has been perceived to be a single problem is discovered to consist of several different problems.)

d. For each potential cause, develop at least 2 potential solutions. (Consider possible effects on customers— safety, cost, etc.)

e. Move to step 4.

Of these, perhaps the most effective is the 4-M Check-list that is shown on the next page.

Another effective tool is the 3 M's: muda, muri, and mura. Are these present in any part of your job? Use the chart on the next page to find out.

The 4M Checklist

Man (operator)	Machine (equipment/ tools/facilities)
1. Follow the established standard? 2. Work efficiency acceptable? 3. Problem (kaizen) consciousness? 4. Reliable? 5. Qualified? 6. Experienced? 7. Training adequate? 8. Assigned to right job? 9. Willing to improve? 10. Maintains good human relations? 11. Healthy?	1. Meets production requirements? 2. Meets process capabilities? 3. Oiling (greasing) adequate? 4. Inspection adequate? 5. Operation stopped often because of mechanical trouble? 6. Meets precision requirements? 7. Unusual noises, vibrations, heat, etc? 8. Is layout efficient? 9. Enough machines/ facilities? 10. Meets safety requirements? 11. Everything in good working order?
Material	**Method (operation)**
1. Mistakes in amount? 2. Mistakes in grade? 3. Mistakes in brand name? 4. Impurities mixed in? 5. Standard in-process stock adequate? 6. Inventory level adequate? 7. Any waste in material? 8. Is handling adequate? 9. Is work-in-process abandoned? 10. Layout adequate? 11. Quality standard adequate?	1. Work standards adequate? 2. Work standard upgraded? 3. Work standardized? 4. Instruction adequate? 5. Method safe? 6. Is it a method that ensures quality product (service)? 7. Method efficient? 8. Is it timely? 9. Sequence or work adequate? 10. Setup adequate? 11. Lighting and ventilation adequate? 12. Adequate contact with previous or next processes?

Typical Analysis Tools

- 4 M's: Man, Machine, Material, Method
- 3 M's: muda (waste), muri (strain), mura (unevenness)
- Flowchart, Cause-and-Effect Diagram
- 5 Why Analysis
- Force Field Analysis
- Checklists, Pareto Chart, Graphs, Histograms

Typical Tools for Potential Solutions

- Brainstorming
- Benchmarking best practice
- Interviewing, affinity diagram

4. Determine root cause and select solutions.

a. Test each potential root cause using the 5 Why analysis. For each problem you ask "why" that condition exists 5 consecutive times.

b. Select the most likely root cause (the potential cause that addresses the most 5 Whys).

c. Clarify what constraints might apply to a proposed solution (approvals required, timing, capital, impact on other parties, etc.). See if constraints eliminate any solutions.

The 3M's

Items to Be Checked	Muda (Waste)	Muri (Strain)	Mura (Uneveness)
1. Manpower			
2. Machines and equipment			
3. Jigs and tools			
4. Materials			
5. Method			
6. Time			
7. Facilities			
8. Production volume			
9. Inventory			
10. Way of thinking			

Developing a List of Ideas

- Is there a better way to do things?
- Can you eliminate a root cause entirely?
- Can you minimize negative forces?
- Can you strengthen positive forces?
- Encourage creative ideas!

What Criteria Will Be Used to Select the Solution?

- Decision must be based on customer requirements first.
- Decision must make sense based on plant's overall strategic plan.
- You can't hurt one operation to help another.

5. Implement solutions.

a. Agree on the action plan for implementation (specific steps, who will perform steps, when, and how).

b. Agree with key decision makers on the circumstances under which implementation will take place. Involve everyone affected by the solution.

c. Monitor and display progress against the implementation plan.

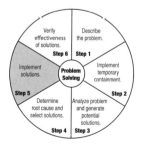

6. Verify effectiveness of solutions.

a. Gather data on the problem. Use a monitoring system, and measurements, to determine if an improvement has been achieved.

  - Has the problem been eliminated? The root cause found and solved? If so, prepare a work instruction, flowchart or other documentation to ensure the solution is standardized. Check to see if any other areas of the plant can benefit from the solution, and share the information with them.

  - If not, has the data improved? Your solution may have failed to eliminate the true root cause. Or you could have addressed the wrong cause or applied an inadequate solution.

  - Has the data remained the same—or grown worse? In this case, none of the actual causes of the problem are being addressed by your solution.

b. If the problem has not been satisfactorily improved or eliminated, return to Step 1!

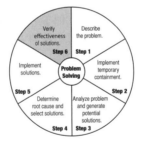

Key Points to Remember

- When a problem occurs, we attempt to fix what we perceive to be the problem. The major concern is to get back on line as soon as possible. "Quick fix" solutions are common. 80 percent of the time companies are fixing the same problem over and over because the true cause has not been identified. Often, that same problem soon returns with root causes seldomly found and few measurements taken.

- The 6-step approach is more disciplined. Follow the steps in sequence. Step 1 is the most important step in problem solving. The key benefits of this 6-step method are:
  - It facilitates a full analysis of the problem or issue
  - It stops you from jumping to conclusions
  - It prevents you from attacking issues that are too big
  - It encourages teams to draw upon the skills, experience and creativity of team members where appropriate, and draw on outside resources when needed
  - It forces you to plan, implement, and evaluate solutions, then "lock in" improvements

- Most failures in problem solving result from improper identification of the problem. If a problem is not successfully solved, remember to check cause and solution. You may have discovered the root cause but applied the wrong solution—or you may have mistaken the true root cause.

Product Quality (PQ) Analysis and Part Routing Analysis

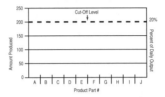

Why use it?

To effectively identify your value stream and ensure kaizen efficiencies.

Who does it?

The manufacturing engineer, manufacturing manager and lean support person, or the cross–functional lean team.

How long will it take to do?

30 minutes to 4 hours. It depends upon the availability of information and whether or not the analysis can be done using a database program such as Access or Excel.

What does it do?

• Quantifies the product and processes and how they relate in a broader picture
• Shows what areas to work on, and why

How do you do it?

Part quantity analysis

Part quantity analysis is a variation of a Pareto chart to examine how the total quantity is distributed among different product types (we assume that larger volume products are the first to be chosen).

The 4 Steps of Part Quantity Analysis

1. List your products along the horizontal axis in order of volume.

2. List the amount produced on the vertical axis.

3. Draw a line indicating products that have over 20 percent of the volume. Any product providing more than 20 percent of total volume should be top priority.

4. Select that product (or products) and apply lean tools.

Example: PQ Analysis

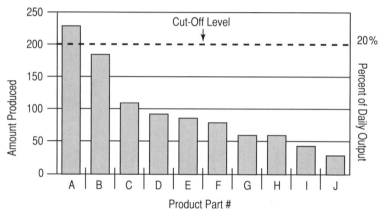

Part routing analysis

If PQ analysis is inconclusive in helping you chose a value stream, you can use product routing analysis. There are 2 methods.

a. Product routing matrix. When the variety of processes and products are complicated, a product routing matrix, sequenced by volume, can be useful. You can see that product A has the highest volume. Products A and D flow through the exact same process. So A and D would be a good choice for a product family or value stream.

Sequenced by Volume

Volume	Product	1	2	3	4	5	6
20,000	A	rc	c	m	d	od	g
12,000	B	rc	c			od	
10,000	C		c	m	d		
3,600	D	rc	c	m	d	od	g
3,300	E		c	c			
3,100	F	rc	c	m	d	od	g
2,600	G	rc	c	m		od	
2,300	H	rc	c	m		od	
2,100	I			c	m	d	
1,000	J	rc	c	m		od	
		1	2	3	4	5	6

Machine

rc = rough cut; c = cut; m = mill; d = drill; od = outside diameter; g = gauge

b. Spaghetti diagram.

- Make a diagram of the factory layout showing operation locations.
- Select a different colored marker for each product.
- Draw the part's travel route on the factory diagram.
- Select the most prominent candidate for improvement from these "spaghetti lines."

Key Points to Remember

- Utilizing part quantity or part routing analysis requires time to collect the data.
- Ensure that everyone is familiar with the product (or product family) upon which focused improvement efforts will be concentrated.
- The more complicated the processing and variety of product, the more time it will take to complete the analysis.
- List external processes (i.e., heat treat, paint, anodize) in the part routing analysis

Quick Changeover (QCO)

Changeover Analysis Chart				
#	Task	Time	Internal	External

Why use it?

To minimize machine downtime due to set-up changeover. Quick changeover is an enabler of many other lean strategies.

Who does it?

Kaizen team with machine operators or set-up crew.

How long will it take to do?

To implement, a 3-day (or less) kaizen workshop would be conducted. Quick changeovers are typically defined to be less than 10 minutes. However, this depends of the complexity of the machinery, the experience of the operators, tooling standardization, and location.

What does it do?

The advantages of quick changeovers are:

- Allows smaller economic lot sizes
- Ability to produce a greater variety of parts
- Reduces in-process inventory
- Reduces lead times
- Minimizes machine downtime

How do you do it?

Changeover time is defined as the time elapsed from production of the last good part prior to changeover to production of first good part after changeover.

1. Determine production requirements for the machine.
2. Videotape and track the changeover or setup. Use a chart similar to the one shown below. This will provide you with an accurate look of what is currently happening.

Changeover Analysis Chart

#	Task	Time	Internal	External

3. Analyze set-up operations and separate the tasks.
   • Tasks that can be done while the machine is running are called *external* operations.
   • Tasks that are completed when the machine is down are called *internal* operations.
4. Move all external operations out of the changeover event.
5. Determine and create the main checklist for the external operations.
6. Determine and create a pre-checklist for the internal operations.
7. Perform basic Workplace Organization and Standardization (5S). (See **5S**)

8. Reduce the remaining internal set-up times.

9. Reduce the external set-up times.

10. Standardize with standardized work.

11. Enforce the standards.

12. Continue to improve.

Seven Tools for Improving Changeover

1. Changeover begins and ends with 5S.

2. Change internal changeover tasks into external changeover tasks whenever possible.

3. Bolts are our enemies.

4. If you have to use your hands, make sure your feet stay put.

5. Don't rely on special fine-tuning skills.

6. Standards are standard: they are not flexible.

7. Standardize all changeover operations, internal and external.

Key Points to Remember

- By preparing and transporting tools and equipment while the machine is still running you can often cut set-up time significantly.
- Moving internal operations out of the machine's downtime can cut changeover time by 50 percent or more.
- If possible, color-code tools for ease of identification.
- Make sure everything needed for a set-up is organized and on hand.
- Organize so that leg movement is minimal and movement of arms is organized.
- Try to eliminate the use of bolts.
- Use dies, jigs, and fixtures wherever possible.
- Time the *entire* changeover, from last good part to first good part.

- Standardize everything and stick to it.
- Utilize quick disconnects when practical.
- Pre-stage tooling.
- Using "kitting" for tooling, gauges, blueprints, routers, etc.

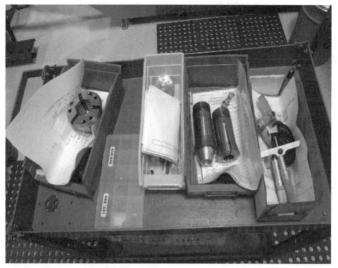

Organizing tools, blueprints, etc. prior to the changeover process will reduce changeovers dramatically.

Consider turret modifications to increase tooling capacity for machining operations.

Runner

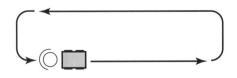

Why use it?

To ensure that takt time or pitch is maintained, and to ensure that value-adding workers focus on value-adding activities only.

Who does it?

The dedicated material handler or the person who has been assigned to deliver parts to the various cells within the value stream.

How long will it take to do?

A runner can be put into place as soon as the runner route and pitch (or paced withdrawal) is prepared.

What does it do?

- A runner, or material handler, levels production by ensuring that the operations have what they need, when they need it.
- The runner (or water spider) allows the line to run at its planned pace.
- The runner is dedicated to the specific work area and is part of the work unit or cell. Runners may supply multiple work areas if time permits.

How do you do it?

1. Begin by studying the future-state value stream map for information. (See **Value Stream Mapping**)
2. Determine the runner's route using paced withdrawal data, takt time data, and pitch data for the target areas.

---

3. Create standard work for the runner's route.

Runner Attributes
- Trained in the value stream production requirements
- Good communicator
- Understands lean concepts
- Understands the importance of pitch and pace
- Is efficient and precise
- Always tries to maintain takt time or pitch

---

4. Create a runner's cart for the route. Make it as small and visually controlled as possible.
5. Train a runner, and a back up, for each shift.

Additional points
- The runner circulates between operations and covers a designated route within the pitch period, picking up kanbans, tooling and components, and finished products and delivering them to their appropriate places.
- If a heijunka box is used, the runner removes kanbans from it to use as visual work orders. If a heijunka box is not being used, then the runner picks up and delivers parts from store locations as required to sustain efficient flow throughout the work areas or cells.
- The runner continuously monitors the functioning of a line or cell as well as pitch. If there is a problem, the runner reports it immediately.

Key Points to Remember

- A runner must:
  - Understand value stream production requirements
  - Communicate well
  - See and report abnormalities
  - Understand lean concepts
  - Understand the importance of, and always strive to maintain, pitch and takt time
  - Work efficiently and precisely
- The runner plays an important role in pro-active problem solving in a lean environment. Since he or she continuously monitors the functioning of a line or cell as well as pitch (or takt time), the runner is closely attuned to how well the value stream is fulfilling its requirements. Thus, the runner is in a unique position to prevent problems that might seriously disrupt production from occurring.
- Remember to allocate time for reloading the runner's cart.
- When you perform line balancing, you can often free up a worker from a targeted operation. This is a perfect opportunity to redeploy that person as a runner.

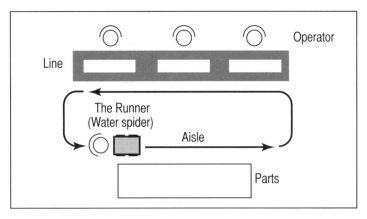

Sequence to Lean Implementation

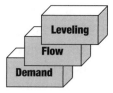

Why use it?

To allow the lean team to systematically identify, analyze, and determine the most effective lean tool to be used at the appropriate time.

Who does it?

Everyone participating on the lean team.

How long will it take to do?

First pass, 1 to 2 hours. However, testing often will have to be completed, and then additional review of the implementation sequence guidelines ensues.

What does it do?

Provides for a structured approach in the implementation of lean tools to ensure a greater chance that improvements will be sustained. It will also:

- Provide a sequence for lean implementation
- Make the team think in terms of the lean implementation sequence of demand, flow, and leveling
- Focus the team on using the right lean tool at the right time

How do you do it?

One of the main reasons lean has not been sustained in many companies is that people "cherry pick" their implementation tools. This is where lean guidelines play an important role.

There is an effective sequence that separates lean implementation into three stages: demand, flow, and leveling. Each stage has tools and methods that make it work. You have the opportunity to customize each stage to fit your needs. Discuss the questions that arise within the team. Solicit their input and gain a consensus. This will be the foundation on which you build your future state value stream map.

Demand phase sequence guidelines

1. What is the customer demand? In other words, what is the takt time?

2. Are you overproducing, underproducing, or meeting demand?

3. Can you meet takt time (or pitch) with current production capabilities?

4. Do you need buffer stock? Where? How much?

5. Do you need safety stock? Where? How much?

6. Will you ship finished goods right after the final station or use a finished goods supermarket?

7. What improvement tools will you use to improve your ability to fulfill customer orders?

Flow phase sequence guidelines

1. Where can you apply continuous flow?

2. What level of flow is needed? One-piece? Small-lot?

3. What type of cell design will accommodate your flow?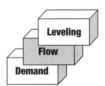

4. How will you control the upstream production? In-process supermarkets? Kanbans?

5. What other improvement methods will help to achieve continuous flow? Quick changeovers?

Leveling phase sequence guidelines

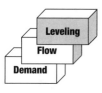

1. What are the minimum lot sizes or days or inventory the system maintains?
2. What types of kanban cards will you use?
3. How will kanbans be distributed and moved?
4. Where in the process will you schedule production requirements?
5. Will you use a heijunka box?
6. What will be the runner's route?

Key Points to Remember

- By mapping the future state, you will identify opportunities to design an efficient, waste-free value stream. The process for mapping the future state takes place in three distinct but related stages, focusing on demand, flow, and leveling.
  - **Demand:** understanding customer demand for your products, including quality characteristics, lead time, and price.
  - **Flow:** implementing continuous flow manufacturing throughout your plant so that both internal and external customers receive the right product, at the right time, in the right quantity.
  - **Leveling:** distributing work evenly, by volume and variety, to reduce inventory and WIP and allow smaller orders by the customer.
- Whenever you make changes, there are two factors that can never be compromised: the customer's needs and safety.

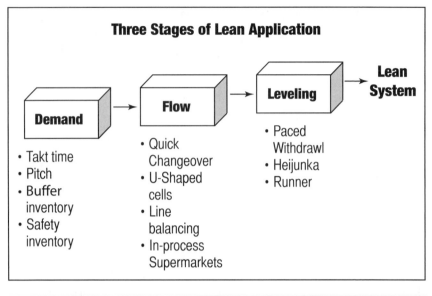

Three Stages of Lean Application

Demand

- Takt time
- Pitch
- Buffer inventory
- Safety inventory

Flow

- Quick Changeover
- U-Shaped cells
- Line balancing
- In-process Supermarkets

Leveling

- Paced Withdrawl
- Heijunka
- Runner

Lean System

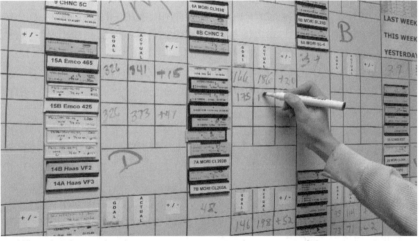

When implementing lean, ensure your people are part of the measurement process. You treasure what you measure!

Six Sigma NEW!

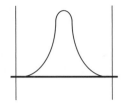

Why use it?

Six Sigma is a sophisticated problem solving approach for improving business performance. Six Sigma is "management driven by data." It is based upon improving processes by controlling and understanding variation, thus improving predictability of business processes. It is a disciplined, data-driven, decision-making methodology.

In its purest form, Six Sigma is a term used to describe a measure of quality control that is near perfection. The Six Sigma process uses data and rigorous statistical analysis to identify "defects" in a process, service, or product, reduce variability, and achieve as close to zero defects as possible.

Less than Six Sigma is not good enough because we would have to accept the following:

- 16,000 pieces of mail lost by the U.S.P.S. every hour
- Two unsafe plan landings per day at O'Hare International Airport in Chicago, Illinois
- 32,000 missed heartbeats per person per year
- 20,000 incorrect drug prescriptions per year in the U.S.
- 22,000 checks deducted from the wrong bank accounts every hour in the U.S.
- 50 newborn babies dropped at birth per day in the U.S.

Who does it?

The Six Sigma process usually is facilitated by a Black Belt trained staff member. Achieving Black Belt certification signifies that the individual has successfully completed an improvement activity with a defined cost savings.

How long will it take to do?

Six Sigma team projects typically will take 1 to 3 months (or longer) depending of the complexity of the problem.

What does it do?

Six Sigma provides the organization with the following:

- Improves internal and external customer satisfaction
- Improves productivity of employees
- Improves problem solving skills
- Reduces costs
- Reduces number of errors or mistakes
- Standardizes continuous improvement methodologies
- Allows for a fact based decision-making process
- Allows for a common language to be used throughout the organization

Six Sigma can be effective when used as part of a business improvement strategy. When combined with the philosophy and methods of lean, it becomes a powerful method for continuous improvement.

Six Sigma is a reference to the goal of reducing defects or mistakes to zero. Sigma is the Greek letter mathematicians use to represent the "standard deviation of a population." The standard deviation from a population represents the variability there is within a group of items, i.e., the population.

Six Sigma is a measure of variation that achieves 3.4 defects per million opportunities, or 99.99966 percent acceptable. It is represented by the following bell shaped curve. The higher the sigma value, the better.

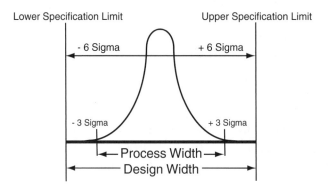

How do you do it?

Six Sigma uses a five-step problem solving tool called **D-M-A-I-C**:

1. **D**efine
2. **M**easure
3. **A**nalyze
4. **I**mprove
5. **C**ontrol

1. Define

Define the customers, their requirements, the Team Charter, and the key process that affects the customer. The following tools can be utilized:

• Team Charter
• Process Mapping
• Cause and Effect Diagram
• Affinity Diagram
• Voice of the Customer (VOC) Table

2. Measure

Identify the key measures and the data collection plan for the process in question. Execute the plan for data collection. The following tools can be utilized:

- Document Tagging
- Data Collection and Check Sheet

3. Analyze

Analyze the data collected as well as the process to determine the root cause(s) for why the process is not performing as desired. The following tools can be utilized:

- Histogram
- Pareto
- Scatter Diagram
- Control or Run Chart
- Design of Experiments (DOE)

4. Improve

Generate and determine potential solutions and plot them on a small scale to determine if they positively improve process performance. The following tools can be utilized:

- Process Mapping or Flowcharting
- Paynter Chart

5. Control

Develop, document, and implement a plan to ensure performance improvement remains at the desired level. The following tools can be utilized:

- Control or Run Charts
- Paynter Chart
- Standard Work

The following is an example of how to calculate the Six Sigma capability for one of your processes:

Six Sigma Calculation Worksheet

Process Name Order Entry   Date 2/06

No.	Action	Equations	Your Calculations
1	What process do you want to consider?		Order Entry
2	How many units were put through the process?		1,283
3	Of those that went through, how many passed?		1,138
4	Compute the yield for the process	= (Step 3) / (Step 2)	.887
5	Compute the defect rate based on Step 4	= 1 - (Step 4)	.113
6	Determine the number of potential things that could create a defect (note: use N = 10 as a conservative number of potential defects)	= N number of critical-to-quality characteristics (CTQs)	10
7	Compute the defect rate per CTQ characteristic	= (Step 5) / (Step 6)	.0113
8	Compute the defects per million opportunities (DPMO)	= (Step 7) x 1,000,000	11,300
9	Convert the DPMO (Step 8) into a sigma value, using a Six Sigma Conversion Chart (google: six sigma conversion table)	Includes a 1.5 sigma shift for all listed values of Z	3.8
10	Draw conclusions		Opportunity for improvement

Key Points to Remember

- Train employees in the various problem solving tools through using actual examples as much as possible.
- The team should utilize a Black Belt for guidance in all phases.
- Compliment Six Sigma projects using lean tools and practices.
- Six Sigma is one tool to be used in an overall business improvement strategy.
- Continue to recognize and reward staff as Six Sigma projects are completed.
- It should be emphasized that to be most effective Six Sigma should be used as part of an overall business improvement strategy, not by itself. When used in this way Six Sigma will become an important and compatible method in your improvement toolbox.

Standard Work

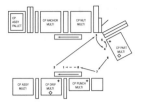

Why use it?

Work must be standardized before it can be improved. This should be used for the basis of all improvement activities.

Who does it?

The lean team works with operators to establish standard work.

How long will it take to do?

1 to 4 hours to create, review and gain a consensus for each form. Complex processes may require much more time.

What does it do?

Establishes the best sequence for each manufacturing and assembly process and establishes a base on which to improve. Standard work consists of a set of procedures that controls tasks so that they are always executed consistently. The work or jobs are organized to ensure all waste is eliminated. Standard work is a major component of kaizen activities because it paces production, helps to eliminate waste and improves upon current practice.

Standard work utilizes two main tools: the Standard Work Combination Table and the Standard Work Chart.

The Standard Work Combination Table:

- Indicates the flow of human work within an operation
- Documents the exact time requirement for each work step or element
- Displays the job design sequence based on takt time
- Demonstrates the time relationship between manual work, machine work, and movement (or walk time)

The Standard Work Chart:

- Displays the work sequence, process layout, and work-in-process
- Displays the operator movement for each work element operation
- Identifies quality, safety, or critical defect areas to monitor

How do you do it?

Standard Work Combination Table

The Standard Work Combination Table is an important tool for the allocation of manpower and allows management to check production volume, judge the skills of each worker, and identify and solve problems. This table clearly shows the flow of human work and automatic feeding through the various steps of a single work process and indicates precisely how much time is needed for each step.

1. Break the tasks for each worker into separate elements.
2. Time each element.
3. Time each walk.
4. Fill out Standard Work Combination Table:
   - list elements and associated items
   - graph each element and walk times
5. Post at job location.

Standard Work Combination Table

		Date:	10/26/02	Needed units per shift	**600**		MANUAL ———
	From Hold out To Set u/p in m/	Section:	**JV**	TAKT TIME:	**54**		AUTO ┄┄┄ WALK

#	Process	Manual	Auto	Walk	Operation time (Unit:)
	WORK	TIME			5 10 15 20 25 30 35 40 45 50 55 60 65 70 75 80
1	Hold outer rail	2	–	1	
2	Set outer rail and outer center pulls multi-welder, and make 2 spot	8	22	3	
3	Hold outer CP and lower	5	–	1	
4	Place outer CP in Part Multi	1	–	1	
5	Hold small part	3	–	1	
6	Set small part in Part Multi-welder start welder	12	21	1	
7	Perform additional spot (5 points) on outer CP	10	–	2	
8	Set outer CP in Punched Multi- and start welder	2	11	1	

Standard Work Chart

The Standard Work Chart illustrates the sequence of the work being performed. This is very useful in worksite management.

1. Draw the cell layout on a chart and label *all* items.
2. Designate work element location by number.
3. Show walking paths with arrows.
4. Fill out all data boxes on chart.
5. Post at job location.

Standard Work Chart

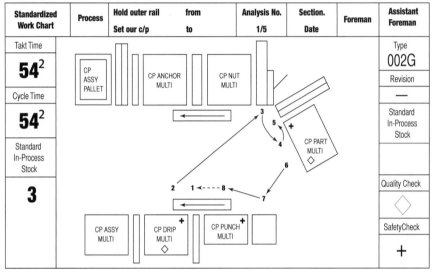

Standardized Work Chart	Process	Hold outer rail from Set our c/p to	Analysis No. 1/5	Section. Date	Foreman	Assistant Foreman

Takt Time: **54²**

Cycle Time: **54²**

Standard In-Process Stock: **3**

CP ASSY PALLET — CP ANCHOR MULTI — CP NUT MULTI — CP PART MULTI — CP ASSY MULTI — CP DRIP MULTI — CP PUNCH MULTI

Type: **002G**

Revision: —

Standard In-Process Stock

Quality Check ◇

SafetyCheck +

Key Points to Remember

- Videotaping can be used to document the current processing sequence. This allows operators to see themselves at work, which frequently brings areas of waste or other problems to their attention. It also provides an accurate time record for each work sequence.
- The Standard Work Combination Table and Standard Work Chart lock in the standard work process and layout for a given job.
- They should be changed only in a sanctioned kaizen event.
- Post the table and chart at the work area.

- Work together with operators to determine the most efficient work methods. Get a consensus, or adherence is unlikely.
- The work standards documented in the table and chart should be enforced to reduce variation. Standardize and stick to it, and you will:
  - improve safety
  - improve quality
  - improve efficiency

Standard work also includes detailed work instructions posted in the work area.

Standard work can include digital photos, along with detailed written instructions.

Storyboard

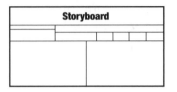

Why use it?

A storyboard is a poster-sized framework for holding all the key information for a lean project. It communicates the progress and key information of a project as it unfolds, so that feedback can be solicited in a timely manner.

Who does it?

1. A project team uses it.
2. Someone is assigned to update it, usually the team leader.
3. Often there will be places on the storyboard where people can make comments, add information, etc. Workers are encouraged to use it.

How long will it take to do?

It lasts as long as the project. It is a living, visual document.

What does it do?

In the case of the value stream management process, or problem solving, the storyboard:

- Visually facilitates the entire process
- Shows the "big picture"
- Shows step-by-step progress
- Helps get buy-in and feedback
- Communicates continuous improvement

How do you do it?

Storyboards are created based on the flow of the steps. It tells the story of what happened in each step.

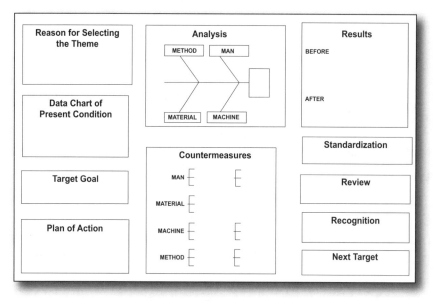

Key Points to Remember

- Trying to incorporate too much information is probably the most common mistake people make with storyboards. Do not forget that the people reading them will not be as familiar with the project as you are and probably will not have very much time to spare. Create the storyboard with that audience in mind.
- Keep the storyboard up to date. As soon as it gets outdated, people will stop reading it—and may never return to it!
- Use colors and photographs to enhance words and drawings.
- Make it poster size and hang it where people will read it.

Takt Time

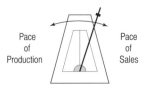

Pace of Production   Pace of Sales

Why use it?

To synchronize the pace of production with the pace of sales. *Takt* is a German word for rhythm, or beat. Takt time is the rate of time needed to produce one quality part to meet customer demand.

Who does it?

The lean team can work with sales to determine customer demand and the level of consistency in the customer's ordering patterns. The team will need to determine manufacturing capacity in terms of man-hours or machine-hours available.

How long will it take to do?

A few minutes to a few hours. The calculation is simple if the customer demand is predictable. If you need to gather historical data to predict customer demand, that may take a few hours.

What does it do?

- Aligns manufacturing rate to customer demand rate
- Focuses awareness on customer demand
- Sets a standard rate that all operations can plan to and be measured against

How do you do it?

The takt time formula is illustrated in the following example.

Example:

$$\textbf{Takt Time} = \frac{\text{Available daily production time}}{\text{Total daily quantity required}} = \frac{\text{Time}}{\text{Volume}}$$

Calculate available work time

Shift 1: 6:00 a.m. to 2:30 p.m. (8.5 hrs., or 510 minutes) with a 20-minute lunch and 10-minute break.

> 8.5 hours X 60 minutes = 510 minutes
> 510 minutes − 20 minute lunch = 490 minutes
> 490 minutes − 10 minute break = 480 minutes
> 480 minutes X 60 seconds = 28,800 seconds

Available work time = 28,800 seconds per shift

Remember to use only available (i.e., paid) work time. Examples of non-production time:

- Lunch
- Breaks
- Meetings
- Scheduled downtime

Calculate customer demand

> 230,400 units historical annual total
>
> 240 working days per year
>
> 230,400 units/240 days = 960 units per day
>
> 960 units per day/2 shifts = 480 units per shift

Remember to calculate for the number of days your operation is working and for multiple shift operations.

Calculate takt time

To determine takt time, divide total number of seconds per shift by customer demand per shift.

$$\textbf{Takt Time} = \frac{28{,}800 \text{ sec. (\# sec. per shift)}}{480 \text{ units (customer demand per shift)}} = \frac{60 \text{ sec.}}{\text{takt time}}$$

Key Points to Remember

- Takt time is the rate at which a company must produce product to satisfy customer demand. Takt time is intended to be the factory or manufacturing pace.
- Takt time sets a regular, predictable pace that forms the foundation for standardized work.
- Takt time must be calculated before standardized work can be planned. Every time takt time changes, standardized work changes.
- Toyota sees the ability to change takt time regularly as an indicator of the maturity of a given facility's lean practices.
- As order volume increases or decreases, takt time may be adjusted so that production and demand are synchronized. As demand increases, takt time decreases.

Part counters at the end of the line where actual is compared to schedule or "takt".

Total Productive Maintenance (TPM)

Why use it?

To improve overall equipment effectiveness and eliminate equipment-related productivity losses.

Who does it?

Project teams made up of production engineers, maintenance staff, line foremen and operators.

How long will it take to do?

Implementing a Total Productive Maintenance (TPM) program for a single machine requires about 2 hours. To do so company wide will take 1 to 2 years.

What does it do?

Total productive maintenance ensures that every machine in a production process is always able to perform its required tasks and, therefore, that production is never interrupted.

Three Goals of TPM

- Maximize effectiveness (overall operating efficiency) of each piece of equipment.
- Provide a system of comprehensive maintenance for the life cycle of equipment.
- Involve departments that plan, design, use and maintain equipment.

How do you do it?

TPM is built on thorough productive maintenance, which adds maintenance prevention and maintainability improvement to conventional preventive maintenance activities. TPM is unique in its use of autonomous maintenance (or operator maintenance) as well as small-group activities to accomplish these goals.

Relationship of TPM to Productive and Preventive Maintenance

	TPM	Productive Maintenance	Preventive Maintenance
Economic efficiency ("Profitable preventive maintenance")	○	○	○
Total system (Maintenance prevention + preventive maintenance + maintainability improvement)	○	○	
Autonomous maintenance by	○		

TPM improvement activities seek to reduce life cycle costs by eliminating the "6 Big Losses." These include:
- Equipment failure
- Setup and adjustment
- Idling and minor stoppages
- Reduced speed
- Process defects
- Reduced yield

TPM activities aim to reduce these losses to zero, to restore plant and equipment to their ideal conditions and to maintain them at that level continuously.

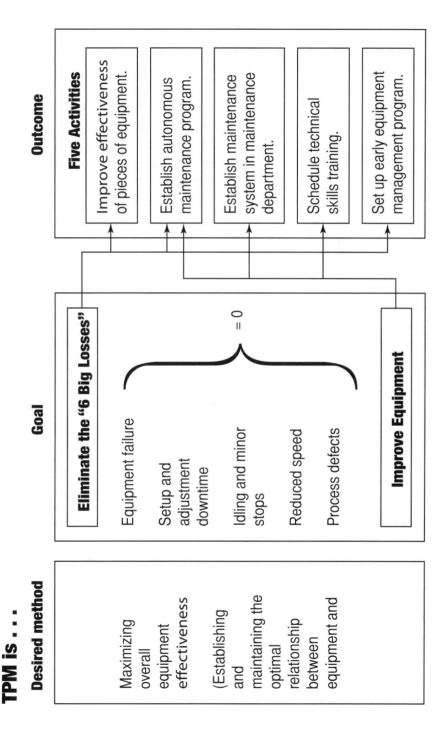

TPM is . . .

Desired method	Goal	Outcome

Desired method

Maximizing overall equipment effectiveness

(Establishing and maintaining the optimal relationship between equipment and

Goal

Eliminate the "6 Big Losses"

Equipment failure

Setup and adjustment downtime

Idling and minor stops

Reduced speed

Process defects

= 0

Improve Equipment

Outcome

Five Activities

Improve effectiveness of pieces of equipment.

Establish autonomous maintenance program.

Establish maintenance system in maintenance department.

Schedule technical skills training.

Set up early equipment management program.

The five activities of TPM

1. **Systematically improve the effectiveness of individual pieces of equipment.** Several project teams choose a process and an improvement focus related to one of the 6 big losses. Each team focuses on a different type of loss, develops improvements and shares its results with other teams. The teams conduct a comprehensive physical analysis of chronic problems ("PM analysis"). Through PM analysis, the team identifies conditions among the causes related to the problem and eliminates them one by one.

2. **Establish an autonomous maintenance program for operators.** Changing the way operators view their own equipment is the first objective in implementing autonomous maintenance. They are taught to clean equipment thoroughly and to take responsibility for it. Autonomous maintenance focuses on maintaining optimal conditions to prevent losses due to breakdowns, speed losses and quality defects by addressing the such abnormal conditions as:
   - Inadequate lubrication
   - Excessive wear due to contamination from grime or the by-products of production
   - Loose or missing bolts, etc.

3. **Set up a planned or scheduled maintenance system in the maintenance department.** Planned maintenance is most effective when the division of work between operators and maintenance personnel is clearly defined and enforced.

4. **Increase operating and maintenance skills through technical training.** This step is essential for effective autonomous maintenance in operations, and for preventive and corrective maintenance in the maintenance department. The training should cover parts common to all types of equipment.

5. **Adopt an early equipment management program for maintenance prevention and maintenance-free design.** In this step, the company works toward the ideal of maintenance-free design. This involves a system of design, testing and feedback that covers the entire life cycle of a piece of equipment.

Autonomous Maintenance Steps

1. Clean and inspect equipment.
2. Eliminate sources of contamination.
3. Lubricate components and establish standards for cleaning and lubrication.
4. Train operator in general inspection of subsystems.
5. Conduct regular general inspections.
6. Establish workplace management and control.
7. Perform advanced improvement activities.

Key Points to Remember

- To fully realize the potential of TPM, everyone in the workforce must change the way they think about equipment. Unless all members of the workforce understand that they alone have the power to eliminate losses, the TPM program will fail.
- TPM changes how people think about equipment, and it involves everyone–from top management to operators—in achieving and maintaining optimal equipment and operating conditions. People are ultimately responsible for equipment operation and maintenance. When workers understand their true role in production, they can begin to eliminate waste and losses by restoring equipment and maintaining it in top condition.

- TPM requires a company wide, team-based effort. Top management must establish clear TPM policies and objectives. Genuine support at the top encourages everyone to develop the skills needed for successful implementation.
- Solid technical training for maintenance personnel is an essential part of TPM development.
- Identification of maintenance can also be a result of a 5S project.

Value Stream Management (VSM)

Why use it?

To ensure lean implementation efforts are identified and sustained over time by linking people and lean tools with measurements and reporting.

Who does it?

1. Everyone participates in the process!
2. A general manager, plant manager or supervisor—with the authority to commit resources to ongoing continuous improvement—must play a leadership role.

How long will it take to do?

3 months to 1 year, then ongoing.

What does it do?

- Links together the metrics and reporting required by managers with the people and tools needed to achieve the expected results
- Provides a step-by-step plan to direct your lean activities, ensuring results are sustainable over time
- Allows you to "see" your work flow and sources of waste
- Determines where to apply lean concepts to improve work flow
- Eliminates redundancies within the value stream
- Maps your future state using lean tools and visual controls
- Installs the appropriate metrics to measure your improvements

How do you do it?

Value stream management consists of these steps:

1. Commit to lean.
2. Select the value stream.
3. Train employees.
4. Draw a current state map.
5. Select metrics.
6. Draw a future state map.
7. Create and implement improvement plans.

1. Commit to lean.

Management commitment and involvement is essential to a lean system. Without it, change will not take place. Management provides the necessary resources for the successful implementation of a lean system, including but not limited to the following:

- Removes departmental roadblocks of territorial nature
- Benchmarks another organization
- Allocates time for training and culture change
- Approves overtime to ensure that team activities for improvement do not interfere with customer shipments
- Attends meetings to show support
- Visits to the floor to see what is being done and to let the team know management is aware of their progress

2. Select the value stream.

A value stream consists of everything that occurs in the completion of a product or service. Value streams can be either manufacturing or administrative based.

A value stream encompasses all the actions (both value-added and non value-added) that are necessary to bring a product from original concept through manufacturing process to receipt of payment. A value stream may include a single process or a linked series of processes. Processes transform material into products; operations are the actions (cutting, heating, grinding, bending, etc.) that accomplish those transformations. The value stream management process helps you systematically identify and eliminate these non value-adding elements.

In many cases, the customer will define the value stream by ordering a product with unique and precise specifications. If they do not, then use product-quantity analysis (PQ analysis) and part routing analysis to chose a value stream to target for improvement. Start with PQ analysis to see if some part numbers are run in volumes high enough to make the choice an obvious one. Use part routing analysis if the results from PQ analysis are inconclusive. (See **PQ Analysis**.)

The appropriate value stream selection depends on your plant and customer demand. Select one that is neither too simple nor too complex.

3. Train employees.

The purpose of Step 3 is to ensure that everyone has a strong understanding of lean concepts and terms for the planning phase. Later, during implementation, you will probably need more training. All companies aspiring to become lean must place a premium on education and training.

To get the core implementation team up to speed, you must develop a workable training plan based on the following 6 steps:

1. Inform all employees about the lean implementation.
2. Determine the required skills and knowledge.
3. Assess current skill and knowledge levels of team members.
4. Determine the gap between present and required skills and knowledge.
5. Schedule the training.
6. Evaluate the effectiveness of the training.

A number of training tools can be applied, including benchmarking another facility that is using lean tools or using books and videos combined with group discussion of the content. It is best to use a variety of materials and resources for the training.

4. Draw a current state map.

The next step is to map current production processes, showing the flow of material and information. This places a stake in the ground and is commonly referred to as the current state value stream, or "process," map. The goal is to gather *accurate*, *real-time data* related to the value stream selected in Step 2. (See **Value Stream Mapping**)

Drawing a current state map will:

- Provide a clear picture of what is currently happening so everyone can gain consensus
- Visually demonstrate what is occurring with the material and information flow using a common set of icons
- Reveal sources of waste

5. Select metrics.

The team is now ready to determine the metrics that will best help them achieve their goals. The metrics may be selected as part of the Team Charter. (See **Lean Communications**)

Lean metrics provide a simple means of demonstrating the impact of the team's efforts as they plan improvement activities, implement them, check the results and make appropriate adjustments, thus helping to drive continuous improvement and waste elimination.

A team needs to identify lean metrics that are clear and that coincide with strategic direction and bottom-line results. The following metrics are typically used within a value stream project:

• Total value stream lead time
• Total value stream cycle time
• Value-added percent
• Defective parts per million or Six Sigma equivalent
• Work-In-Process as expressed in days-on-hand or turns
• Scrap
• First-run yield

6. Draw a future state map.

The next step is to design the future state of your value stream. You will draw a future state map in detail. Mapping the future state is done systematically, using a "3S" approach: stability, standardization, and simplification.

By mapping the future state you identify opportunities to design an efficient, waste-free value stream. The process for mapping the future state takes place in three stages, focusing on:

1. **Demand**—understanding customer demand for your products, including quality characteristics, lead time, and price
2. **Flow**—implementing continuous flow manufacturing throughout your plant and offices so that both internal and external customers receive the right product, at the right time, and in the right quantity
3. **Leveling**—distributing work evenly, by volume and variety, to reduce inventory and WIP, and allow smaller orders by the customer

7. Create and implement improvement plans.

Improvement plans should be derived from the maps created in Step 6. Improvement activities range from simple adjustments to a total rearrangement of equipment and people in the plant. Any activity that improves the process or area can be viewed as an "improvement event."

Broadly detail the improvement events that need to occur and have them reviewed by management prior to implementing the improvement plan. Once a consensus has been gained for the overall value stream improvement initiatives, utilize a storyboard (and/or lean reporting forms/templates) to ensure that effective communication occurs throughout implementation.

Improvement Milestone Chart

Value Stream: _____ Date: _____ Page ___ of ___

Event	Task	Duration	Person	Weekly Schedule											
				1	2	3	4	5	6	7	8	9	10	11	12
5S	Sort	2 months	D.T.												

As you implement your future state, things will change and you will most likely have to modify your plan. There may be many iterations of your future state. Overall, you must develop the mindset to look for and eliminate non value-added activities (i.e., waste).

Lean is a never-ending journey, a continuous effort that allows organizations to become world-class. Organizations must meet the following criteria:

1. Operate by the cost reduction principle
2. Produce the highest quality in their business sector (i.e., zero defects)
3. Meet quality, cost and delivery requirements (i.e.,100% On-Time-Delivery)
4. Eliminate all waste from the customer's value stream

Key Points to Remember

- Acknowledge the necessary resources at the beginning with the Team Charter.
- Continue to communicate even if progress seems slow.
- Remember, value stream maps are very similar to Team Charters—they are living documents that will change as conditions change.

Value Stream Mapping

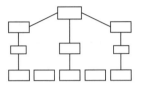

Why use it?

To allow a team to easily "see" the material and information flow for a product family and subsequently utilize lean tools to eliminate waste.

Who does it?

A cross-functional team made up of production, material planning, and quality personnel.

How long will it take to do?

1 to 2 days. As you gain more experience with mapping, the process will become easier.

What does it do?

- Creates a common vision for everyone connected to the targeted value stream, of both current and future states
- Provides a visual map for ease of communications
- Allows waste to be seen by everyone so improvements can be focused
- Provides the foundation on which to base lean initiatives from the customer's perspective

Value stream mapping is the visual representation of the material and information flow of a specified product family. It is very useful *within a systematic approach to lean implementation*. This mapping tool originated with Toyota and has found success within manufacturing operations worldwide.

Do not utilize it exclusively as a management tool—get all your key people involved, and share the maps with everyone in the plant. Everyone involved in the process will come to visualize the big picture, and from there advance to finding sources of waste and eliminating them.

How do you do it?

Value stream mapping is of two types: current and future state. Create the maps on whiteboard, or on a flipchart, so that all workers and managers involved in the targeted value stream can easily see and decipher them.

The current state map

Value stream mapping begins with the current state and proceeds according to the following steps.

1. Gather as much data as possible.

2. Review the basic production steps before going to the shop floor or process steps if mapping an administrative value stream.

3. Communicate to all areas the purpose and activities of the team.

4. Utilize icons to draw a "shell" of your current-state map listing the main processes, supplier, customer, production control, and/or any external outsourcing.

 Dedicated process box—the main process area where value-added and possible non value-added activities occur (welding, assembly, machining, painting, etc.).

Shared process box—where multiple value streams are scheduled (paint, anodize, deburring, etc.).

Attribute area—particular features/ characteristics of the process (cycle times, line speeds, number of operators, changeover times, etc.).

Customer or supplier—the most upstream and downstream customer with their respective attributes.

 Truck shipment—denotes the physical arrival or departure of parts from the supplier, customer or external outsourcing location.

 Inventory—the amount of customer days-on-hand of inventory in process.

 Database—computer interaction (EDI, E-commerce, etc.).

→ *Manual information flow*—physical conveyance of information (routers, schedules, mail, etc.).

 Electronic information flow—the electronic signal that communicates information (orders, schedules, shipments, etc.).

X *Exceptions or disruptions*—any major obstacle that prevents flow from occurring throughout the value stream.

 "Go-see scheduling"—the physical viewing of material to determine if more product is required.

➡ *Push*—the movement of product or material downstream regardless of need.

◯ *Worker*—the operator(s) assigned to the particular process.

5. Go to the shop floor, department, or area, beginning with the most downstream process (i.e., shipping) and collect the actual process attributes of cycle times, changeovers, line speeds, uptime, number of operators/workers, inventory amounts, work-in-process and so on for each process.

6. Gather data where it exists—on the floor or in the area, not from memory or sitting in the meeting room.

7. Introduce yourselves to workers in the area, show them what you are doing, ask them questions and get them involved. If you need to time a changeover or a process cycle time, explain to the operator why you are doing this and ask for their approval.

8. Use as much "real" data as possible, or use an average from the last 3 months

9. Everyone should visit the floor, area, or department.

10. Identify attributes for each process/location and show them on the map. However, note only the process, not the exception to the process, on the map.

11. When drawing flows, draw *both* material and information flows. Think in terms of upstream and downstream flow.

12. Away from the shop floor or area, discuss the data that has been collected. If you do not gain a consensus at this step, you may be forced to make changes another day. Do not rush this step!

13. Enter the data under the processes on the current state map.

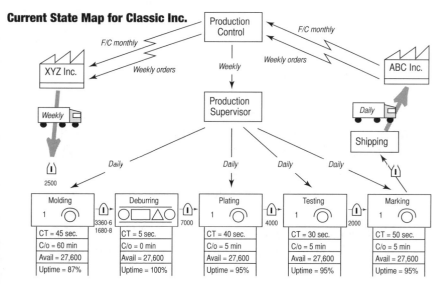

Current State Map for Classic Inc.

14. Draw all forms of communication, electronic, and/or manual.

15. At the bottom of the map, convert amount of inventory (Work-In-Process) to days and cycle times to a step graph.

16. Total days of inventory and cycle times to arrive at total lead time.

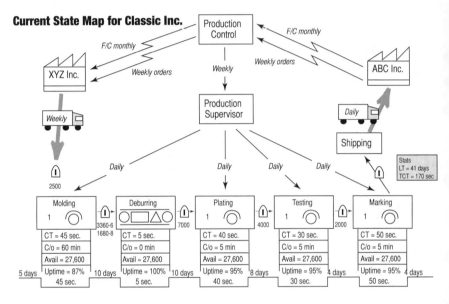

The future state map

The future state map is completed in three stages. The first stage is to determine how to meet customer demand. The second is to create continuous flow and a pull system. The third stage is to achieve load leveling (heijunka).

1. Utilize the demand future-state icons and draw the demand future-state map.

 Buffer inventory—the amount and location of inventory required due to variations in customer demand.

 Safety inventory—the amount and location of inventory required due to internal inefficiencies.

Supermarket—a limited amount of inventory controlled by kanbans. Nothing moves in or out without a kanban.

Future State Map for Classic Inc.

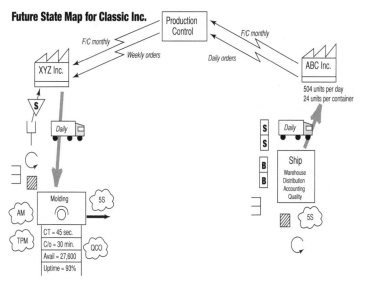

2. Utilize the flow future state icons and draw the flow future-state map.

 Production kanban—the signal used within a pull system that represents a certain amount of material/parts to be produced by the upstream process.

 Withdrawal kanban—the signal used within a pull system that represents a certain amount of material/parts to be withdrawn from a super-market (or process) by the downstream process.

Signal kanban—the signal used within a pull system that represents a material lot that needs replenishment by the upstream process. Typically used for machining to determine most efficient changeovers.

Kanban post—the physical location where kanbans cards are placed in order to be picked up by the upstream process or customer.

 U-shaped cell—the physical arrangement of workers and/or work elements in a counterclockwise arrangement for ease of product movement.

 Physical material pull—the physical removal of product from the downstream process to provide for continuous flow.

Max = XX
□○△ *FIFO lane*—a pre-determined amount of inventory between processes that adhere to First-In-First-Out material flow.

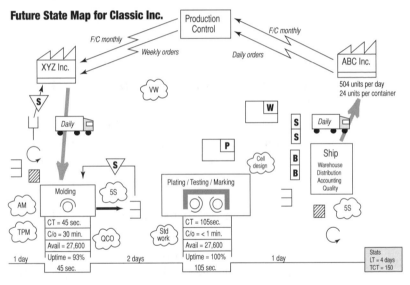

Future State Map for Classic Inc.

3. Utilize the load leveling future-state icons and draw the load leveling future-state map.

 Heijunka box—the physical device holding the kanbans for the day that have been scheduled by customer(s) volume and variety product needs. Pitch increment required.

 Runner—the worker who delivers inventory to the cells and units Just-In-Time.

Kaizen focus—the specific area of focus for the value stream to attain the future state.

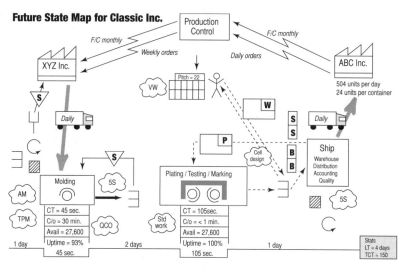

Future State Map for Classic Inc.

Review maps with everyone associated with the proposed changes. Post maps, metrics, and timelines on communication boards. Update as events occur and metrics improve.

Key Points to Remember

- Value stream mapping is a valuable part of a systematic approach to lean implementation. It should not be used in isolation.
- Get key people involved and share the map with everyone— not just management.
- Create the current and future state maps on whiteboard or a flipchart so that all can see them.
- You can create a great map, but follow-through is more important—have the right people involved and ensure that there is communication and ongoing implementation.
- Always draw the customer first, then the supplier, then the processes. Uses individual process boxes when drawing the maps and are separated by the queue times and delays that occur.

- The best value stream maps will not be implemented and sustained if the key workers are not involved in the mapping process, proper communications does not occur, and management does not show support. Keep these in mind when creating the action plans for implementing the future state.

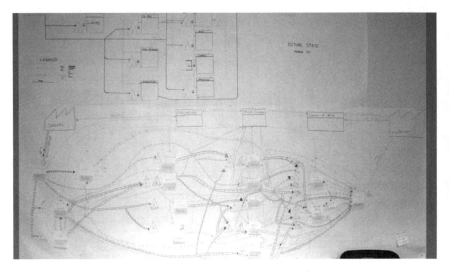

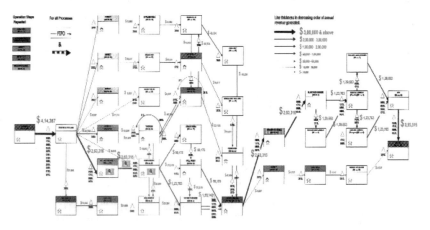

Value stream maps will come in all shapes and sizes.

Visual Factory

Why use it?

To establish a system of visual communication and control throughout the plant. In fact, the visual factory operates at the highest level of the 5S concept, visual control.

Who does it?

A cross-functional visual factory team drives the project, with help from target area teams throughout the plant.

How long will it take to do?

Approximately 6 months for a mid-sized plant (250,000-sq. ft.).

What does it do?

- Standardizes the 5S system throughout the plant
- Standardizes visual metrics throughout the plant
- Standardizes visual displays throughout the plant
- Standardizes visual controls throughout the plant

How do you do it?

You will create a visual language that can be used plant wide, using the following steps:

1. Form and train the visual factory team.
2. Create an implementation plan.
3. Create standards for visual displays and controls.
4. Begin implementation.
5. Ensure 5S system implementation and standardization.

6. Standardize visual metrics.
7. Standardize visual displays.
8. Standardize visual controls.

1. Form and train the visual factory team.

This will be a cross-functional team responsible for plant wide implementation. It is their job to:

a. Create a visual factory vision and plan.
b. Create visual display and control standards.
c. Form and train target teams.
d. Help target teams implement visual metrics (VM), visual displays (VD), and visual controls (VC).
e. Ensure standardization of 5S system, visual metrics, visual displays, and visual controls.

2. Create an implementation plan.

To create an implementation plan you must designate target areas, name a champion for each area and decide when you will attempt to implement each visual factory activity. A typical planning form is shown below.

Visual Factory Worksheet

Team Leader _____ Date _____

Eval. Date	5S Completion Date	VM Completion Date	VD Completion Date	VC Completion Date

3. Create standards for visual displays and controls.

The visual factory encompasses all lean activities—workplace organization, cell design, kanban, supermarkets, Jidoka, equipment maintenance, and quick changeovers. It also plays a major role in planning, using storyboards, standardized work and value stream mapping as its primary tools. Therefore, a great deal of time and money can be saved if the visual factory team designs and standardizes displays and controls.

Example:

Below is an example of a visual control, in this case a safety stock kanban card, that is self-explanatory regarding standards and procedures.

Removal from Safety Stock Inventory

When you remove this container from the safety inventory, notify the appropriate authority!

Fill out the Safety Stock Log.

Please give this Safety Stock Kanban to the department manager.

Removal from Heijunka Box

Please place this Safety Stock Kanban into the container and place the container in the safety stock in date rotation order.

---

4. Begin implementation.

When you begin working in target areas you will find that some go quickly, others do not. Among the visual displays and controls that can be implemented on a plant wide basis is the signboard strategy.

The signboard strategy

Just as one would become exasperated trying to find an address in a town with no street signs; in an office or factory without signboards only the most experienced employees would know where to find things. Everyone else would be at a loss.

To turn a factory into a workplace where one can see where everything belongs, at a glance, we need a "facility address" system and a signboard strategy.

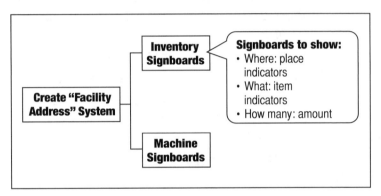

5. Ensure 5S system implementation and standardization.

The 5S system creates the foundation for a visual factory. (See **5S**)

6. Standardize visual metrics.

Effective use of information depends on effective reporting and display of information. Visual metrics can be very helpful in the overall implementation of a lean system in that they:

- Make data easy for teams to understand and interpret
- Focus improvement activity
- Keep everyone up to date

Characteristics of Visual Metrics

The bar chart below is a good example of a visual metric, because it has the following characteristics:

- It is directly related to strategy
- It is a non-financial measure
- The measure is location-specific
- The measure will change over time (At some point, it may not be necessary to measure the shipment of this particular product.)
- It is easy to use
- It provides fast feedback
- It fosters improvement

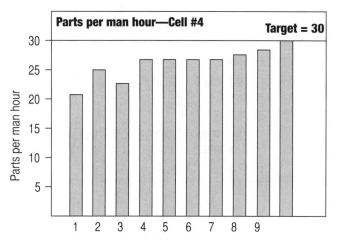

7. Standardize visual displays.

Visual displays communicate important information about the work environment, safety, operations, storage, quality, equipment, tools, improvement activities, and other work standards.

8. Standardize visual controls.

The idea is to integrated a process to ensure there is no deviation from the standard. The following table recaps the various tools available for you to achieve this.

Visual Control Tool Categories

Type	General Purpose
Storyboards	To share information about projects or improvements.To educate and motivate.
Signboards	To share vital information at point of use.
Maps	To share actual processes, standard operating procedures, directions, etc.
Kanbans	To control the withdrawal of inventory (or tools) in and out of supermarkets, lines and cells. It can also be used to regulate orders from the factory to suppliers.
Checklists	To provide an operational tool that facilitates adherence to standards, procedures, criteria, etc.
Indicators	To show correct location, item types, amount, direction or proper motion by building that information into the workplace.
Andons/Alarms	To provide a strong or unavoidable sign when there is an abnormality or action to be taken.
Mistake-Proofing	To prevent abnormalities or problems from occurring or from moving to the next process or step.

Key Points to Remember

- The visual factory begins with a simple premise: one picture is worth a thousand words. If that picture is available exactly when you need it, where you need it, with just the right amount of information, then it's worth several thousand words.
- Visual display and control are part of all lean activities.
- The visual factory begins in the first minute of lean planning and implementation, and continues throughout continuous improvement. Put another way, a lean factory is a visual factory, and the essence of the visual factory is Just-In-Time information.
- Be diligent about posting visual signboards in the workplace.

Visual displays should be located at point-of-use, as well as color coded (legend, upper right).

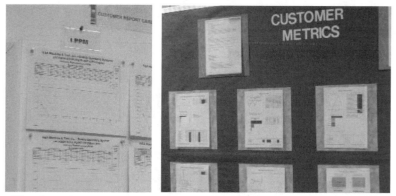

Visual metrics come in all shapes and sizes. Ensure they are up-to-date and easy to understand.

Waste

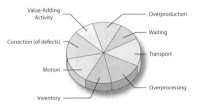

Why use it?

The goal of lean is to identify, analyze, and eliminate all sources of waste in all operations.

The work cycle

The work cycle is useful for developing an understanding of waste and as a visual display to show before-and-after kaizen events. All operations consist of 3 elements:

- Waste
- Incidental work
- Actual work

Waste—work that is unnecessary and adds no value

Incidental work (Auxiliary work)—work that is required to support value-added work but does not necessarily add value

- Grasping tool and moving it to the fastener
- Placing part in position prior to fastening
- Filing a customer report

Actual work—operations or steps that add value to the product or service

- Machining of material
- Assembly tasks
- Entering customer order

Who does it?

Everyone in the organization must be involved in the identification and elimination of waste.

How long will it take to do?

This process is never-ending—the elimination of waste is the foundation of continuous improvement.

What does it do?

Becoming waste free:

- Reduces cost to the organization
- Reduces time to process
- Adds quality to products
- Adds to your production capacity
- Gives you a competitive edge

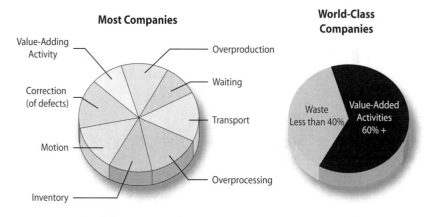

How do you do it?

The process of waste elimination can be applied to countless applications. By eliminating waste step-by-step you will cut costs significantly. Toyota originally defined 7 types of waste to target and eliminate.

The 7 Deadly Wastes

1. Overproduction
2. Waiting
3. Transport
4. Overprocessing
5. Inventory
6. Motion
7. Correction (of defects)

1. Waste of overproduction

Overproduction is the worst of all wastes. It is producing more than is required to meet customer demand or producing it at a faster pace than is necessary. Overproduction hides 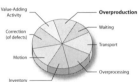 production problems or defects, workload fluctuations and production inefficiencies. It opens the door for other kinds of waste.

Why does overproduction exist?

The root cause of overproduction is that machines and workers have excess capacity (waste) and put this excess capacity to work to turn out excess product. But a lean manufacturing system controls over-production by "pulling" and producing only what is needed to ship, using tools such as kanban and paced withdrawal.

To detect this waste, ask:

- Is production faster or slower than takt time?
- Is there inventory in queue waiting for processing?
- Is there lack of one-piece flow or small-lot flow?
- Can material presentation be improved?
- Is scheduling based on production quotas?
- Is there a lack of a pull system?
- Is takt time being used?

2. Waste of waiting

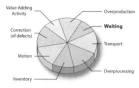

Waiting for anything—people, material, machines or information—is waste. Waiting means idle time—and that causes the workflow to stop. The waste of waiting is "low-hanging fruit"—easy to get a hold of and ripe for the taking. In addition, it will lead you to other problems that you did not know you had.

To detect this waste, ask:

- Am I always watching the same operation and not adding any value?
- Can something else be completed during waiting time?
- Is standardized work being followed?
- Is there a pull system in place?
- Are there buffers between processes? Are they in the right quantity?
- Is the kanban calculation correct?
- Does transport time vary considerably?

3. Waste of transport

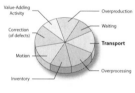

Transport is an important element in production, as it affects the delivery of all parts and materials. But transporting goods further than necessary, or temporarily relocating and moving them, is waste. Likewise, any conveyance not required for Just-In-Time production is a form of waste—it adds no value from the customer's standpoint. Minimize all transport by locating sequential operations as close together as possible. Transport that cannot be eliminated should be automated.

To detect this waste, ask:

- Are parts/supplies moved and stored in inventory?
- Is plant and office layout optimized?
- Is transfer of parts fully automated?

---

4. Waste of overprocessing

Putting more work or effort into a part than is required by the customer is waste. Excessive processing does not add value for the customer and the customer will not pay for it. This is the most difficult of the wastes to uncover.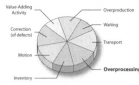

To detect this waste, ask:

- What is the basic function of this procedure or part?
- Is this process design poor?
- Are there incorrect machine or process capability specifications?
- Is there a clear understanding of customer requirements?
- Do part specifications match customer requirements?

5. Waste of inventory

Excess stock of anything is waste. Inventory takes up space, may impact safety, and can become obsolete if work requirements change. Using a pull system, takt time or paced withdrawal will reduce inventory waste. Everyone in the plant must have a basic awareness of the problem of waste inventory and also must have the tools to do something about it.

To detect this waste, ask:

- Are there queues everywhere?
- Are parts purchased or machined in larger quantities than customer demand?
- What is the amount of obsolete inventory?
- Is process capability poor?
- Is there a lack of properly sized and placed buffers?
- Is there standardized work, and is it being followed?
- Is there a lack of confidence in one-piece or small-lot flow?

6. Waste of motion

Any movement of people, material, or machinery that does not add value is waste of motion. This type of waste can be created by poor equipment layout or poorly placed parts, dies and tools, causing more walking, reaching, or bending than necessary.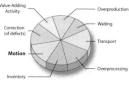

To detect this waste, ask:

• Can walking be reduced?
• Can body movement at any tasks be reduced?
• Can items be moved closer to the worker?
• Can the workstation benefit from cellular layout?
• Are proper kaizen techniques in use?
• Is there a thorough 5S program?
• Is standardized work being followed?
• Is cross-training being done?

7. Waste of correction (of defects)

This category of waste refers to all processing needed to correct defects. Defects result in additional time, materials, energy, capacity and labor cost. Lean has advanced from inspections that just separate the good from the bad 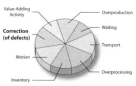 to inspections at the source that build quality into each operation. In addition, mistake-proofing and Jidoka have built-in automatic methods of detecting and preventing defects.

To detect this waste, ask:

• What is the defect rate?
• Are there common reasons for defects?
• Are master parts available?
• Is inventory hiding the defects?
• Is there a lack of process capability of machine, tool or techniques?
• Is standardized work being followed?

(8.) The Waste of People's Skills (People Utilization)

Also you will find at times an eighth waste of people utilization. This waste does not use people's skills to their fullest.

This was a quick review of the wastes. Consider the following questions:

1. How can I start to communicate about these wastes through-out the organization?
2. What are some low-hanging fruit?
3. What can be done immediately to improve customer satis-faction?

These types of questions should stimulate similar questions and allow more open communications regarding waste.

Cost reduction principle

Most companies find that only about 5 percent of their activities are value-added. The rest are non value-added—wasted activity. *To be world class, an organization must operate at a level of 60 percent value-added activity, or higher!*

Management is under constant pressure from the customer to reduce costs while maintaining the highest quality. Traditional thinking dictates that you set your sale price by calculating your cost and adding on a margin of profit. But today's market is so competitive that the customer sets the price. You no longer have the luxury of adding a margin of profit. Under these circumstances, the only way to remain profitable is by eliminating waste, thus reducing costs.

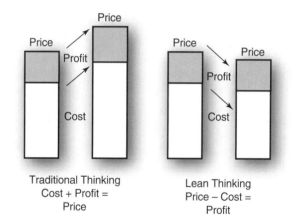

Traditional Thinking
Cost + Profit =
Price

Lean Thinking
Price – Cost =
Profit

This is called the cost reduction principle. It states that:

a. Customers determine price by what they are willing to pay.
b. You as the producer determine your own cost by how much waste you are willing to tolerate!
c. What is left over is your profit.

In brief: eliminating waste is the primary means of maximizing profits!

Key Points to Remember

- Waste is anything that does not add value in your customer's eyes and for which they are unwilling to pay.
- You must learn to view waste a new set of eyes, and as you increase your awareness of what actually constitutes waste, then work to eliminate it.
- Most organizations react only to waste on a large scale. In lean thinking, identifying and eliminating many small instances of waste can lead to a large overall change.
- The ultimate lean target is the total elimination of waste.
- Eliminating waste saves money only if the worker effort previously expended in a wasteful activity is redirected into value-adding activity. This principle is known as "converting waste to work." It is essential for becoming a world-class company.

Waste Audit NEW!

Use the following four pages as a guide to conduct a Waste Audit for the area that is being improved. A Waste Audit should be completed once a value stream current state map has been created. Workers should go to the area and ask similar type questions that are contained in this audit.

If some team members are not familiar with the area or process being improved, it is recommended that a brief tour be conducted prior to creating the current-state value stream map.

The Waste Audit is meant to provide awareness to obvious waste. The application of the lean tools will eliminate the waste identified. Frequently teams too quickly apply a lean tool and do not fully understand how it should be used. By correctly and accurately identifying the specific waste, the lean tool application will be that much more effective.

Waste Category	Definition	Examples
Overproduction	This waste is producing more work or providing a service prior to it being required. That is the greatest of all the wastes. In that, if you overproduce some type of work or service, it encompasses many of the other wastes.	Push production methods Production not in sync with planning Long setups Extra inventory on hand Materials not presented on time Producing reports no one reads Entering repetitive information
Waiting	Waiting for anything (i.e., people, material, machine availability, information, etc.) that is excessive is waste. Waiting means idle time - and that causes work flow to stop. The waste of waiting is "low-hanging" fruit - because it is easy to get hold of and ripe for the taking.	Work piece delays from upstream process Missing items Worker absent Work not moved to next process in efficient manner Lack of standard work Buffers not used Kanban calculation not correct Excessive signatures required Dependency on others to complete task Lack of planning Lack of understanding of downstream process needs
Motion	Any movement of people, material, paper, electronic exchanges (E-mails, etc.) that does not add value is waste. This waste can be created by poor equipment or office layout or design, not effective equipment, supplies located afar, etc.	Searching for tools or supplies Searching for prints Searching for computer files on your desktop Inefficient cell or office layout Excessive walking between processes Searching for work documents (files) Reviewing manuals for information Hand-carrying paper work to another department or process
Transport	Transport is an important and ubiquitous element. It affects the delivery of any work. It is the movement of any work or material that does not add value. Any conveyance not required for Just-In-Time production can be considered waste.	Inefficient plant and office layout Partial part completion moved to storage location Lack of machining flexibiliy Excessive filing of work documents E-mail distribution lists that are not up-to-date

To Detect This Waste Ask	Notes for Your Target Area
Is this product or work being produced to a schedule or a customer demand? Is pull being used to move material or work between processes? Are parts, materials, administrative work group in small lots if one-piece flow is not practical? Is excess inventory because of long setup times? Is leveling being used?	
Are there delays in the delivery of material or information? Are there issues with punctuality with internal as well as external customers? Are there certain times where delays are more prevelant? Is there a bottleneck in the process? If so, where and why? Have delays always been a problem or is it a recent development?	
Can walking be reduced by repositioning equipment and/or supplies? Is the information and/or material (i.e., prints, gauges, tools, etc.) to do the work easily accessible? Are new and current employees properly trained in the process? Can tooling or information required to do the job be accessible within 5 seconds? Are prodedures in place for all critical processes? Are there certain areas that impede work flow?	
Is the information or work that is being transformed being hand delivered to other processes? Is work being delivered to the right place at the right time? Has work been consolidated, where appropriate? Are kanbans being used? And if so, have they been reviewed as to how many are needed?	

Waste Category	Definition	Examples
Overprocessing	Putting more work or effort into the work required by the internal or external customer is waste. Excessive processing does not add value for the customer and the customer will not pay for it.	Customer specs have not been thoroughly reviewed Poor process design Incorrect information being shared Unnecessary testing or inspection Duplicative documentation
Inventory	Excess stock of anything is waste. It takes up space, may impact safety, and can become obsolete if work requirements change. Using a pull system, takt time, and/or paced withdrawal will reduce inventory waste.	In-process stocking locations being used due to long set-ups Material purchased only due to large quantity discounts No one-piece or small-lot flow Process capability poor Ineffective use of buffer and safety stock Inventory stacks block walkways
Correction (of defects)	Correction (of defect) waste refers to all processing required in creating a defect and the additional work required to correct a defect. And defects (either internal or external) result in additional administrative processing that will add no value to the product or service. It takes less time to do work correctly the first time than the time it would take to do it over. Rework is waste and adds more cost to any product or service. This waste can reduce profits significantly.	Customer complaints Customer returns No self-inspection Wrong parts used No human automation Human error Standard work not available Process not reviewed Product design poor Data entry errors Pricing and quoting errors Lost files/records
People's Skill	Many times this is the 8th waste. The underutilization of people is a result of not placing people where they can (and will) use their knowledge, skills, and abilities to their fullest. Use company policies and procedures to effectively place people where they will most benefit the organization.	Project deadlines not being met Work loads not evenly balanced due to lack of cross-training High absenteeism and turnover Incomplete job skill assessment prior to hiring Little contributions to improvement initiatives

To Detect This Waste Ask	Notes for Your Target Area
Has the basic function of the part been reviewed for process improvements? Are the specifications up-to-date? Has someone confirmed that this is exactly what the customer needs in reference to finish, film, etc.? Has this process been reviewed within the last six months?	
Are there containers in the walkways or boxes sitting in offices? Are you using the hall for storage? Are there excess finished goods stored in the area? Are internal or external customers waiting for information or a service to be provided? Is everyone working to their full capacity? Are setup times being reduced plant wide? Are customers and suppliers on kanbans?	
Are there well-documented standard processes? Does equipment have a maintenance schedule? Are customer complaints and returns a major impact on the organization? Are there effecitve cross-training programs? Do employees have the proper amount of time to do their work error-free? Is Poka-Yoke being used where there are problems or potential problems?	
Are employees effectively cross-trained? Are employees encouraged to suggest improvements? Are employees empowered to implement improvements? Are new employees trained to best practice?	

Glossary NEW!

5S - A process to ensure work areas are systematically kept clean and organized, ensuring employee safety and providing the foundation on which to build a lean system.

Active State - The horizontal position of a file folder indicating work needs to be completed.

Activity - The single or multiple act on taking a course of action.

Assessment - A structured form upon which to analyze a department or area relative to a particular topic.

Benchmarking - A structured approach to identify, visit, and adapt world-class practices to an organization.

Brainstorming - The process of capturing people's ideas and organizing their thoughts around common themes.

Buffer Stock - Stock that is made available between processes to meet takt time due to variations in upstream or downstream cycle times.

Catchball - The back and forth communication between levels within an organization to ensure team alignment.

Cause and Effect Diagram - The visual representation to clearly display the various factors affecting a process.

Continuous Flow - A processes' ability to replenish a single work unit or service that has been requested or "pulled" from a downstream process. It is synonymous with Just-In-Time (JIT), which ensures both internal and external customers receive the work unit or service when it is needed, in the exact amounts.

Check Sheet - The visual representation of the number of times an activity, event, or process occurred for a specified time period.

Control Chart - The visual representation of tracking progress over time. Similar to line graphs.

Cycle Time - The time elapsed from the beginning of a work process request until it is completed.

Customer Demand - The quantity of product or service required by the customer. Also referred to as takt time.

Data - Factual information used as a basis for further analysis.

Document Tagging - The physical attachment of a form to a process work unit to document dates and times.

First-In-First-Out (FIFO) - A work controlled method to ensure the oldest work upstream (first in) is the first to be processed downstream (first out).

Fishbone Diagram - *See Cause and Effect Diagram.*

Flow - The movement of material or information.

Frequency Chart - The visual representation of the number of times an activity, event, or process occurred for a specified time period.

Heijunka - *See Leveling.*

Heijunka Box - A physical device to hold the work units arranged by value streams. Similar to a group of mail boxes.

Histogram - The visual representation that displays the spread and shape of the data distribution.

Individual Cycle Time - The rate of completion of an individual task or single operation of work.

In-process Supermarket - The control of work units in and out of an area residing between two processes to improve work flow.

Interruption - Stopping of a process without notice.

Leveling (same as Heijunka) - The balancing of work amongst the workers during a period of time both by volume and variety.

Jidoka - The concept to achieve the appropriate level of automation that detects defects and/or halts a process when a defect is found.

Just-In-Time (JIT) - Synonymous with continuous flow. It is the provision that the process or customer is supplied with the exact product or service with the right amount at the right time.

Kaizen - "Kai" means to "take apart" and "zen" means to "make good." Kaizen is synonymous with continuous improvement.

Kaizen Event - A focused group of individuals dedicated to applying Lean tools to a specific area within a certain time period.

Kanban - A card or visual indicator that serves as a means to communicating to an upstream process precisely what is required at the specified time.

Lean Office - The administrative area working systematically to identify and eliminate all waste.

Metric - A specific number (data) that is utilized to measure before and after improvement initiatives.

Meeting Information Form - The document to effectively manage meetings, detail agendas, and list action items.

Mistake-proofing (Poka-Yoke) - The design and use of error prevention to achieve zero defects.

Office Layout - A self-contained, well-occupied space that improves the flow of work and data transactions. This would include software requirements.

Paced Withdrawal - The scheduling of work to be removed from a process at a certain time.

Paper File System - The arrangement of administrative work such that it is organized and processed quickly.

Pareto Chart - The visual representation in a bar chart format listing issues in descending order of importance.

Passive State - The vertical position of a file folder indicating work has been completed.

Pitch - The adjusted takt time to move work units throughout the value stream.

Predictable Output - The assurance that a work unit or service will be exactly what is expected.

Problem Solving - A team working together, following a structured process, to remedy a situation that caused a deviation from a norm.

Process - A sequence of tasks (or activities) to deliver a product or service.

Process Folder - The specific information and detailed flow for a particular process.

Process Mapping - Visual representation of a sequence of operations (tasks) consisting of people, work duties, and transactions that occur for the design and delivery of a product or service.

Process Master Document - The listing of all processes within a department or value stream.

Production Kanban - A printed card indicating the number of parts that need to be processed to replenish what was taken.

Pull - A system in which nothing is produced by an upstream (supplier process) until the downstream (customer process) signals the need for it. This enables work to flow without detailed schedules.

Push - Work is pushed along regardless of need or request.

Queue Times - The amount of time a work unit or service request must wait until it is released.

Quick Changeover - The process to reduce the time elapsed from the production of the last good part to the production of the first good part after a new setup.

Red Tag - A label used in the 5S process to identify items that are not needed or are placed in the wrong area.

Resistance - The opposition of an idea or concept.

Root Cause - The origin or source of the problem.

Runner - A designated function for someone to maintain value stream pitch integrity.

Safety Stock - Stock that is made available to protect takt time (i.e., customer ordering patterns).

Set-In-Order - The second activity in the 5S system. This will ensure items are properly stored and placed in the correct location.

Shine - The third activity in the 5S system. This involves cleaning everything thoroughly and ensuring cleaning is part of the audit process.

Six Sigma - A sophisticated problem solving methodology.

Signal Kanban - A printed card indicating the reorder point has been attained and a particular material lot needs to be replenished.

Sort - The first activity in the 5S system. This involves the weeding out of items within the target area that have not been used for a period of time or are not expected to be used.

Standardize - The fourth activity in the 5S system. This involves the creation of documents/rules to ensure the first 3S's will be done regularly (and made visible).

Standard Work - This is a process to gather the relevant information to document the best practice of producing a work unit or providing a service. It should be the basis for all continuous improvement activities.

Standard Work Combination Table - The visual representation displaying the flow of human work and all the various steps required to complete a process.

Standard Work Chart - The visual representation displaying the sequence, process layout, and work units for a process.

Status Report - The document that details the team's progress to date, as well as issues and plan(s) to keep on track.

Storyboard - A graphically rich, visual representation of a Lean or problem solving project that displays critical information. Storyboards can be 8.5" x 11" or can be poster size.

Supermarket - The system of storing a certain level of in-process work or service capacity to be pulled by the downstream customer when there is a difference in the cycle times of the process(es).

Sustain - The fifth activity in the 5S system. This involves the process to monitor and ensures adherence to the first 4Ss. Many times this will be a regular audit.

System Folder - The "keeper" of all pertinent information about the processes within a department or value stream.

Takt Time - The pace of customer demand. Takt time determines how fast a process must run to meet customer demand.

Task - A single event within a process.

Team Charter - A document detailing the team's mission and deliverable to ensure strategic alignment.

Total Cycle Time - The rate of completion of a process or group of tasks that have a common element. It is calculated by adding up the individual cycle times for that process or value stream.

Toyota Production System - The compilation of world-class practices documented by the Toyota Motor Corporation. It is synonymous with lean throughout the world.

Value-Added Time Reporting Log - The document to track the process cycle times.

Value Stream - A sequence of processes that are connected by a common customer, product, or service request.

Value Stream Management - The process of lean implementation to link the metrics and reporting required by managers with the people and tools needed to achieve the expected results.

Value Stream Mapping - The visual representation of the processes (work units and information required) to meet a customer demand.

Visual Control - The visual indicators used to ensure a process produces what is expected, and if not, what must happen.

Visual Metric - The display of measurements.

Visual Factory - The ability to convey all relevant information about a product or service by the means of signs, posters, or anything that appears to the eye.

Waste - Anything that adds cost or time without adding value. The seven most common wastes are: 1) Overproduction, 2) Waiting, 3) Transport, 4) Overprocessing, 5) Inventory, 6) Motion, and 7) Correction (of Defects). Many times you will see an eighth waste added, that being 8) People Utilization.

Withdrawal Kanban - A printed card indicating the number of parts that need to be removed from the supermarket and supplied downstream.

Work Load Balancing - The distribution of work units across the value stream to meet takt time or pitch.

Work Unit - A specific, measurable amount of work that can be segmented and/or treated as a whole.

The New Lean Pocket Guide XL
Instant Suggestion Form

Remove this sheet from the book and hand it into your lean facilitator or whomever is responsible for implementing suggestions.

Present Condition: _____

Suggested Improvement: _____

_____

_____

The New LPG XL **Page Reference:** _____

Anticipated Results: _____

Improvement's Impact on Work Environment:

_____

_____

_____

_____

_____

Initiator's Name: _____

Contact Name: _____

Supervisor's Approval: _____

Date Submitted: _____

Phone Ext. and E-Mail: _____

Date Accepted: _____

The New Lean Pocket Guide XL
Instant Suggestion Form

Remove this sheet from the book and hand it into your lean facilitator or whomever is responsible for implementing suggestions.

Present Condition: _____

Suggested Improvement: _____

_____

_____

The New LPG XL **Page Reference:** _____

Anticipated Results: _____

Improvement's Impact on Work Environment:

_____

_____

_____

_____

_____

Initiator's Name: _____

Contact Name: _____

Supervisor's Approval: _____

Date Submitted: _____

Phone Ext. and E-Mail: _____

Date Accepted: _____

The New Lean Pocket Guide XL
Instant Suggestion Form

Remove this sheet from the book and hand it into your lean facilitator or whomever is responsible for implementing suggestions.

Present Condition: _____

Suggested Improvement: _____

_____

_____

The New LPG XL **Page Reference:** _____

Anticipated Results: _____

Improvement's Impact on Work Environment:

_____

_____

_____

_____

_____

Initiator's Name: _____

Contact Name: _____

Supervisor's Approval: _____

Date Submitted: _____

Phone Ext. and E-Mail: _____

Date Accepted: _____

The New Lean Pocket Guide XL
Instant Suggestion Form

Remove this sheet from the book and hand it into your lean facilitator or whomever is responsible for implementing suggestions.

Present Condition: _____

Suggested Improvement: _____

_____

_____

***The New LPG XL* Page Reference:** _____

Anticipated Results: _____

Improvement's Impact on Work Environment:

_____

_____

_____

_____

_____

Initiator's Name: _____

Contact Name: _____

Supervisor's Approval: _____

Date Submitted: _____

Phone Ext. and E-Mail: _____

Date Accepted: _____

Customization of The Lean Store Products, Videos, and Books

Customize The Lean Store products, videos, and books with your company's name and logo, mission or vision statement – or anything else that is unique to your company.

Benefits of customization

- Allows for greater flexibility in determining specific content
- Helps the company focus on key areas or concepts
- Communicates your company's commitment to the lean movement
- Creates a shared vision throughout the company

Additional details

- Please allow 2 weeks for delivery of customized products, videos, and books
- Customization with your company logo on the covers for quantities of 50 or more
- Products, videos, and books can be translated into other languages
- Full license of the products, videos, and books can be made - just contact us and ask

Visit The Lean Store
www.theleanstore.com

**for all your continuous improvement needs.
Each month new products, books, videos, and
worksheets will be made available as self-help
tools for you to use!**

**Also, check out the Just For Fun section of the
store.**